One Percent Inspiration, 99 Percent Desperation

Mark Patinkin

Covered Bridge Press
North Attleborough, MA

DEDICATION

For Wayne Brasler, who taught me to do and love this work 30 years ago.
I've never had a better teacher.

Covered Bridge Press
7 Adamsdale Road
N. Attleborough, MA 02760

(508) 761-7721

ISBN 0-924771-63-1

Printed in the United States of America

10 9 8 7 6 5 4 3 2 1

Contents

INTRODUCTION

You don't want to live with a newspaper columnist. I had just opened the mirror above the sink to retrieve a toothbrush.

"You sleep well?" my wife asked.

"I've got it," I said.

"Got what?"

"I'll bet I'm not the only one who looks in other people's medicine cabinets. That sound like a column?"

She asked if I ever think of anything besides what to write about for the next day's paper.

Not often. Which is how I ended up with the title for this book. People who write columns are sometimes asked where they get ideas. We like to say it's inspiration, but in truth that's about 1 percent of it. If I didn't have to write three columns a week, I would probably write one a month. Which is to say about 99 percent of ideas come from desperation, when the clock is ticking, and you've got to find 70 lines for tomorrow somewhere, anywhere.

I've been perfecting this approach to deadlines since school. I never finished a term paper earlier than the night before it was due. Well, that's exaggeration. Sometimes it was the morning of.

That's not to say this job is a burden. It's easier than most, certainly other journalistic work, and I'm lucky to have it. I'm the person who always wanted to be a fireman and became one. Seventeen years ago, during a lapse in judgment, the editor of the Providence Journal gave me a chance to try writing a column. I've written about 3,000 in that time, God help my paper's readers. From all that, I figured there would be enough passable ones to fill a book, but in sifting through them I got a rude wake-up. Just about all that I considered the better ones had problems.

Many who collect their articles in book form let them stand as written. If there were flaws, fine, that's the nature of daily or weekly journalism: Done under the gun. Such writers have healthier egos than I do. In this collection, I decided to try fixing the flaws. Some pieces were just touched up, others reconditioned, virtually all were changed at least slightly. I did a fair amount of cutting back. That was painful, you never want to lose something you've created, but I kept reminding myself of the solitary word Clint Eastwood is said to use when giving advice to actors he's directing in a movie.

"Less."

It took a longer time than I imagined to do the fixing up, and I'll never again say anything bad about editors. Fixing up is what they do for a living. It's harder than writing.

This brings up some people I'm indebted to. I've worked with some fine editors over the years, and all had a hand in helping save me from myself. Jack Monaghan was my first column editor, tough but fair and still both those things. John Granatino and Andy Burkhardt have done tours dealing with my copy, bless them. Most recently my partner-in-crime has been Alan Rosenberg, who seems to care about my work as much as I. At the Scripps-Howard News Service, I had the luck of hooking up with Walter Veazey, a man with a gift for encouraging writers. Then there are the big bosses in *the Providence Journal* newsroom, who have always given me enough rope to do my damage: Jim Wyman, Joel Rawson and Carol Young. I'll never forget Chuck Hauser, who in 1979, for better or worse, offered me this assignment. And there are the two principals of Covered Bridge Press, who are taking the chance that someone other than my mother will buy this book: Chuck Durang and Doug Paton.

Finally, Hemingway said a writer should not write for the widest possible audience, but rather for the one person you love. For the last dozen years, I've tried hard to take his advice. And so:

To Heidi, the greatest thanks.

OF BACON LOTS, COLD-SLAW AND ROMANTIC FEVER

A while back, a young boy made national news when he saved the life of a choking playmate by using the Heimlich maneuver. Doctors said he did it perfectly. He was not as successful at remembering what it was called.

He referred to it as the Time-Life Remover.

We shouldn't be too hard on him. Word mangling is a common affliction.

For a number years, I used to catch butterflies in the bacon lot at the corner of my block. It was an overgrown tract filled with tall underbrush. Until I was about 10, I was convinced that somewhere beneath the ground in there, strips of bacon were growing, like carrots. Companies such as Oscar Mayer, I presumed, had dozens of laborers who would be sent to bacon lots around the city to harvest the strips and put them in cellophane packages. I wondered why I never saw those workers in my own bacon lot. I was shocked when someone finally explained to me about pigs.

One of my favorite dishes as a child was cold slaw, called that because it had to be refrigerated. I also liked catch-up, so named because it took so long to make it out of the lip of the bottle.

When I was 6, I had romantic fever. I was too young at the time to think it was linked to romance, as I didn't know what romance was, but it soon became clear that romantic fever had something to do with your mother being on the verge of tears, taking you to a toy store and saying you could buy anything you wanted. I hoped at that point I would get Romantic Fever as often as possible, though I changed my mind when I found it also involved penicillin shots.

I hated penicillin shots. They hurt much more than the tennis shot I was given a year before after cutting myself on a rusty playground slide.

I got over romantic fever, but resented having to take sulfur pills for the next decade, as I didn't think it was wise to put all that sulfur into my system, especially after I got a chemistry kit and saw that sulfur was toxic.

It wasn't until my late 20s that I found a reference to a drug called Sulfa, and started to think.

My brother Douglas was also given to word problems. For years, he was under the impression that the Great Stock Market Crash could only mean that the roof of the exchange building had suddenly caved in, killing hundreds and sending the country into a tailspin. He pictured businessmen in top hats lying amid the rubble.

My wife had a stock market misconception of her own. When she would hear radio reports of hectic chair-trading, she had visions of a huge auditorium filled with chairs that were bought and sold by frantic brokers. She was not sure why this occurred.

She was also unsure why things got misty outside whenever the frog rolled in. Frogs did not seem large enough to her to create atmospheric change.

On the other hand, she found it logical that lobbyists were given that name because they stood in lobbies while negotiating with senators.

Her sister had a harder time when she had to sing a certain hymn with a line about "Bringing in the Sheets." Not realizing that sheaves were bundles of wheat, she concluded that even in biblical times, there was such a thing as laundry day, when everyone stripped their beds. She presumed it was a pretty sacred event or else they wouldn't have written a hymn about it.

Word-mangling can skew our grasp of history. I knew of someone who, until he was 10 or so, thought it was the Silver War, and that Abraham Lincoln's contribution to the ages had to do with his resolving a dispute over precious metals.

Speaking of politics, my 7-year-old daughter, until just the other day, pictured candidates for high office lining up in jogging shoes, since the White House is turned over each election year to the fastest runner in the Presidential race.

Then there's the Pledge of Allegiance, responsible for many children having a mistaken view of America as a nation both underground and invisible. I remember a former colleague once writing about her own word-mangling; in her childhood, she used to love the early morning light, since it was so dawnserly, much like the light in the Star Spangled Banner.

There are variations on word-mangling that lead to other kinds of misconceptions. A woman colleague remembers being confused as a child when her parents would offer guests a drink.

"No thanks," many would say, "I don't drink." She didn't know how they were able to survive.

I have since resolved my own misconceptions and do no more word mangling that I know of, which means my view of the world is more accurate today.

But somehow, life seemed more interesting when I was able to go to sleep at night knowing that a new crop of bacon was growing beneath the empty lot at the corner of the block.

AT LEAST THEY'LL KNOW HER VOICE

The weather was cold for Florida, in the 50s, and the Gulf was coming hard onto the beach. It did not look inviting, especially so early, 7 a.m., with the light just beginning. But I was here only a few days, and I did not want to miss the water. Besides, if you can force yourself, it's a good way to wake up.

It was just before the New Year and we were staying in a condominium complex. We had come down so the children could see their grandparents. They're retired now and spend winters here.

The rest of the time they are near Chicago, where I grew up. I left in 1970 for college, and the roads that opened up to me never led back. I found a new place to call home. Most of my friends did the same. It's not the 50s anymore; moving from your hometown is common. It was only after having children that I began to see how much you give up.

The grass was cold and full of dew and it appeared I was the only one outside. Then I got to the beach, where the complex had recliners lined up, and suddenly heard a voice.

I turned and saw an odd sight. A few yards away, a middle-aged woman was reading a book out loud. All by herself.

I took a quick swim and didn't think much more about it until the next morning. The same woman was there again, still reading out loud. I wondered whether she was a bit off.

Then I saw she had a tape recorder. She was reading into a microphone. That explained it, somewhat. Maybe she was a reader for those books-on-tape. No, couldn't be, not with loud surf in the background. Maybe she was reading for the blind. Or practicing elocution. Or something.

Finally, when I saw her a third time the next dawn, I got bold and asked.

She clicked off the recorder and gave me a warm smile.

"This can be embarrassing," she laughed. "I never know what people think."

Then she explained.

"I'm reading to my grandchildren."

She had two of them. She said they lived out west, far from her Ohio home. Her daughter had moved there, and she doesn't get to see them much. So she's developed a ritual: Every day, she reads a story, and sends the tapes out in bunches. That way, each night, the two children can go to sleep with their grandmother reading to them.

She said her daughter scolds her whenever she reads long stories, because that keeps the kids up late. But she does it anyway—this morning's book was taking 45 minutes—because it means they spend more time with their grandma.

I don't think you'd have found many grandmothers doing this kind of thing 25 years ago. There wasn't much need. I was typical, I grew up within 10 minutes of all my grandparents, and within a half hour of nearly all my uncles, aunts and cousins. Most kids I knew were similar. I doubt most kids are today.

I recently finished writing a small book, and at store signings in my adopted state of Rhode Island, it seemed that half those in line were buying for adult children who had moved far away. To personalize each book, I would ask what their kids and grandkids were up to. They would tell me, and add how proud they were of the things their children had achieved, but I would often see longing in their eyes.

"Think they'll ever move back here?" I'd ask.

"Oh no," they'd quickly answer, as if guarding against getting their hopes up. "They love where they are. It's good for them."

Most people who have had children, and perhaps most who haven't, understand that your role is to teach them to fly, not hold on.

It's just hard when they fly so far. And harder still when they start raising their own children in a distant place. There aren't many guidebooks on how to be a grandparent from 1,000 miles away. You have to figure out new ways to connect as you go along.

Which is why some people are willing to get up every morning, in the near-dark and cold, to read stories for grandchildren into a tape recorder.

They may not even recognize her when she sees them next, the woman on the beach told me. But at least they'll know her voice.

IN THE FAR EAST THEY HAVE A NAME FOR PAIN: MASSAGE

Time to head down to the hotel's massage room. I won't feel guilty about it, either. It's the end of my second week on business in the Far East, and the stress of the road is getting to me. I deserve some pampering. Besides, I've never had a massage before; not a professional one.

I'll give Hong Kong's Regent Hotel credit, they don't go cheap on the decor: a marble-walled massage room. Very nice. I'm feeling relaxed already. A young Asian man greets me.

"You may hang clothes in closet," he says.

I'm new at this.

"How much of my clothes?"

"All clothes, please."

"Uh, you got a towel or something?"

Of course there's a towel. I'm embarrassed for being so uptight. "Nothing better than a real massage," people have told me. "You'll never feel more relaxed." I'm ready. Relaxation, here I come.

Gently, the masseuse takes my left arm. Suddenly, not so gently, he grinds the heel of his hand against it. Then he starts jamming the muscles into places they've never been before. He seems to hit a new nerve center every few seconds. I'm not speaking here of discomfort, I'm speaking of pain.

I try to remain calm. "I think I'm a little ticklish there," I say.

"We just begin," he says. "You relax, yes?"

He's right. I'm here to unwind. It's all in how you look at it. This isn't pain, it's release. A gentle massage would be useless. I've got to trust it. I've got to welcome it. The harder the better.

He grabs the little finger of my left hand. What's he going to do now? What he does is pull it—a short, sharp pull that makes it crack. Then he does it to the next finger. And the next.

"Excuse me sir," I say, deferentially. ``Is this what everybody gets?"

"Yes. We are cracking you out. Yes?"

I don't want to be rude. I clench my teeth until he's finished. I'm beginning to get a headache. At least he's done cracking me out. No he isn't. Now he moves to the other arm.

"Actually," I say, "that arm feels fine."

"Excuse me, sir. This your first time, yes?"

"Yes."

He smiles. "Ahhh. First time. It's okay. You feel better afterward."

He's right, of course. It's my fault, not his. A massage is all in the mind. If I decide to enjoy it, I'll enjoy it. I've got to think East—think release, not pain. Nothing will feel better than getting my right hand cracked out, too. He starts in on it. I pull it away.

"I hurt hand in tennis," I lie. "Hand injured. Bad injury. Nasty, really."

He tries working on my neck instead, then stops and taps it.

"You must relax," he says. "You are tight like wood here, yes?"

If some sadist cracked you out, you'd be tight like wood, too.

"Sorry," I say.

The neck done, he walks to the other end of the table and rakes his hand from my heel to my thigh. It makes my body tense up like an ironing board. He keeps doing it though. I'm soon so tense, so arched, I'm rocking on my belly like a seesaw.

"Take easy, take easy," he says. "You are like flying banana, yes?"

"Aren't most people?"

"No, no, no. Most, they sleep."

I'm as likely to sleep through this as gum surgery. My headache's getting worse. He moves to the other leg. Wait a minute. I think I know what's going on here. This guy isn't Hong Kong Chinese. He's North Korean. He's trying to get me to talk. Well I won't talk.

He starts cracking out my toes.

I'll talk. If he'll stop, I'll tell him anything he wants to know.

"You go to school for this?" I ask.

"What you think, I make it up?"

A tactical error. I've got him upset. Calm him down or I've had it.

"What I mean is, it must have been a very good school."

Hold it. What's he doing, now? He's climbing onto the table. He's grabbing some ceiling bars, lifting himself, and no, wait, I can't believe this. He's grinding his heel into my back. Now both heels. Now he's walking on my back. I mean really walking. I can picture my ribs buckling. I can picture the headline. "American Turned Into Quadriplegic by Massage."

"Maybe not so rough," I say.

"You feel better afterward. Most sleep through this, yes?"

He lifts himself on the bars, both feet off the table, then comes down on either side of my back, heels first, letting them grind down my sides.

Somebody, please, call the police. I'm being killed. I'm being murdered by a lunatic.

"This okay?" he says.

"Fine. Great."

Thank goodness. He climbs off the table. I just lie there, tight as a drum all over. I'm a nervous wreck. I haven't had this bad a headache in months.

"One last," he says.

Then he grinds both hands into my temples. Forget aspirin, I want morphine.

"It over. Now you feel better, yes?"

Better? I'm going to count ten, man, and then I'm going to break both your arms.

"Yes. Much better. Thank you. Thank you very much. It was terrific."

Some advice. Next time you want to pamper yourself in Hong Kong, order room service.

🕐

THE REASON THEY FOUGHT

He was sitting in the bleachers, third row up. Across the gymnasium, he watched the graduates enter through the door. Gil Woodside was in his mid-40s and a high school social studies teacher. This day, three of his Vietnam veteran friends were with him. It was important to him that they witness this together.

Soon, among the other graduates, he spotted her. "That's the girl," Woodside said. His veteran friends strained to see. "That pretty Asian girl," said Woodside. "That's Ahn Le."

None of the four said anything. They just looked.

How long since he'd been over there? More than 25 years. He was 19 when he enlisted in the Marines, April of 1965. It was a family tradition. Woodside's father had been in World War II, his grandfather a cavalryman in World War I. He'd been raised to see his freedom as special, and feel a debt to defend it.

He arrived in Vietnam early in the war, when there was still idealism. But sitting now in the gymnasium, he remembered the difficult times, too. He remembered Lopez, the young Navajo. They used to play cards and read each other's letters. They would joke about how they'd shared so much they could find the bread in one another's kitchens back home. Then, one day, Lopez went out on patrol in an armored personnel carrier, and there was a direct hit, and the memory of that loss has never left him.

There was also the memory of the helicopters coming in, the first time he ran to help take the wounded to triage, lifting a stretcher, seeing what had happened to the soldier's stomach, then seeing the corpsman next to him trying to push something back inside.

And then the most painful memory: Seeing the war go bad after he got home. He'd been proud of helping the Vietnamese stay free, and now it was ending with footage of U.S. helicopters in retreat, leaving the people behind.

It left something unhealed in him; in most veterans, really. For Woodside, it was symbolized by the way, back in the States, veterans would shy from the Vietnamese who had come here, as if they felt they'd let them down.

It was about three years before when a colleague told him about the new girl at the high school, an immigrant from Vietnam named Ahn Le. Woodside decided to reach out. Over time, they began to talk. She told him about her family, produce merchants near Saigon. She told him about Communist rule, how her parents, seeing no future, left everything, first becoming boat people, then refugees, finally immigrants, and at last, for Ahn Le, only months ago, Americans.

And now graduation. Soon it was over. Students and parents mingled in the school foyer. Slowly, with his friends following, Woodside threaded his way to Ahn Le. He found her standing with her family. He introduced the others—fellow veterans, he explained. They'd fought in Vietnam, too. They had believed in helping the people there stay free.

Each of the men congratulated Ahn Le. Then Woodside spoke.

"What do you think, guys?"

They nodded. "Sure."

The four of them fell into a disciplined line, at rigid attention. They faced Ahn Le. She stood there in white cap and gown.

Woodside gave a crisp order.

"Hand salute."

The four snapped their right hands to their foreheads. They stood that way for a good five seconds, emphasizing their respect. At last, another order: "Ready to."

Hands down.

He will always remember the tears in the eyes of the girl's grandmother, and the thank yous from all of them.

Afterward, the four veterans were alone, and all shared the same thought: That they'd fought to bring the Vietnamese opportunity, and on this day, for this one girl, they'd seen it happen. They'd seen one small harvest of their sacrifice. And in that moment, at least for Woodside, something inside him began to heal.

WHILE WE'RE AT IT, LET ME TELL YOU ABOUT MY MALADY

I've just discovered the most dangerous phrase in the language for anyone doing home decorating.

"While we're at it . . ."

After buying a house a few months ago, I decided to turn a third-floor room into a study. The room was fine except for a crack in the ceiling over the staircase. I figured a few hundreds dollars would take care of it. I lined up a contractor.

He came by to see the crack. Then, briefly, we talked about what else was possible. Large mistake. When you're fixing up a house, never talk about what else is possible.

"You know," I said to the contractor, "if this is going to be a study, I sure could use some more storage." I asked him about building cabinets into the walls, to take advantage of the dead space.

Good idea, he said. About $600.

I decided to allow myself this one indulgence.

Then I made another mistake. I invited over a decorator. It wasn't a business visit, she was a friend, but she brought with her something that while-we're-at-it sufferers should not be around: Good taste. We're very susceptible to suggestion.

"You know," the decorator suggested, "this room would really be spectacular if you tore out the ceiling and made a cathedral effect."

"I don't know," said my wife, "that could be expensive."

I've always wanted a study with a cathedral ceiling. "You're right," I said to my wife. "But if we're going to do it ever, it would be cheaper now. I mean, while we're at it."

The workmen began to tear out the ceiling. I went up to see how it looked. There's a second smaller room on the third floor I'd presumed we'd use for storage. But then I began think. Tear out that ceiling, too, and it would have possibilities. The builder looked it over and said I'd sure get some bang for my dollar. A cathedral ceiling, he said, would transform this into a cozy guest bedroom.

"Well," I said, "while we're at it."

That night, my wife played out her gender role by asking how much the work in the second room would cost.

"It'll only be another $800 or so," I said. Sufferers of this syndrome always use the word ``only" before mentioning money.

"But we don't have another $800 or so."

There's another thing people like me are good at, rationalizing. I did some quick figuring and then glanced up triumphantly. Look at it this way, I told her: If we paid that off over a year's time, it would only be $15.38 a week.

That sounded good to her, which brings up yet another aspect of this syndrome: It's communicable, especially between spouses.

We went ahead. I began to do something else sufferers of this syndrome should avoid: Hang around the work space during construction. This is bad for you as it only gives you ideas.

I got the idea of a skylight. You really can't have cathedral ceilings without one.

Great idea, said the contractor. About $700.

"Well," I said, "as long as we're at it."

They cut in the skylight near the ceiling's peak. It looked terrific up there. It would have looked almost as good at eye level, but I had to make a choice, so I put it high. Of course, a second skylight at eye level would be nice, but it would cost too much. Besides, they'd already nailed in the insulation. We couldn't start tearing that up to indulge ourselves in another skylight. I put it out of my mind.

I couldn't put it out of my mind. I couldn't sleep nights. I would spend long minutes hanging around the work space, picturing it. I wanted another skylight. It was more than wanting it; if I was going to do work up there, I needed it.

This is still another phase of the syndrome—you move from "I want it" to "I need it." Finally comes, "I deserve it."

"What have we done to deserve it?" said my wife.

That's when I went to the while-we're-at-it fallback defense.

"We'll get it back," I said.

"Pardon?"

"If we ever sell the house, we'll get it back."

She asked: But where are we going to get the money now?

I tried the "we'll-regret-it-if-we-don't" rationalization. "Five years from now," I said, "we'll look back and say we should have done it then when a skylight cost half as much."

"They cost $700," she said.

I did some quick figuring. "But if we pay for it over a year," I said, "it would only be $13.46 a week."

We put in the extra skylight.

Then I had them put in a third—made sense since they were already at it.

Just as we were finishing, I got another idea. The room sure would look nice if we rounded off the top of the front window with one of those half-circle panes of glass. Of course, that would mean cutting a hole in the wall and reshingling the outside. The builder said it could cost over $1,000 for such an add-on, and it would make very little difference.

"But as long as you're here," I said.

That's when he sat me down and told me my malady was getting out of hand. He'd seen this before, how homeowners lost all perspective. There comes a time, he said, when you have to stop. The room, he assured me, was perfect; don't overdo.

That helped. I agreed that enough was enough. "It is perfect, isn't it?"

He nodded, adding that the only small flaw, was that you had to bend over slightly while walking up the stairs because of the slope of the roof, but that's common. No big deal. Consider this job perfect, he said.

I do. But I've been thinking. If we added one more skylight over the stairs, it would solve that problem. And it's not just that I want it; we need it. Deserve it. And now's the time. While they're here.

While we're at it.

🕐

THE GRADUATE

Her son was still asleep when Karen Singleton walked into his room. On his desk, she noticed the alphabet puzzle he had been working on the day before, and his new Peter and the Wolf book; first-grade reading level. Gently, she shook her son awake.

He is 21 years old.

"Happy Graduation Day," said Karen.

Andrew Singleton smiled but did not respond. His weakest skill is speech. He is only able to say limited phrases. His mother sat on his bed. "You're going to graduate today," she said. "You're going to have a high school diploma." She talked about the special center he would go to afterward to learn job skills.

"Graduate," said Andrew. He seemed to understand.

He went into the kitchen for breakfast, then back to his room. Karen soon followed. Andrew still needs assistance getting dressed and washed, but she was surprised to find him in the shower, the water just right, shampooing his hair. She called to her husband, a doctor. "Did you put him in the shower?"

No. He hadn't. Neither had Karen's two teenage sons. She stood there a bit overwhelmed: This was a first for him. It was the kind of moment that made her realize how good for him it had been to enroll two years ago in the town high school, in Middletown, Rhode Island. It gave him the confidence to feel grown up.

Andrew is 4-foot-11 with brown hair and brown eyes. In addition to the retardation, he has deformities in his legs that make it hard for him to walk more than short distances. Around noon, the youngest of his two brothers helped put his wheelchair into the family's Jeep Cherokee and they all headed to school.

On the way, Karen thought about the last two years. Andrew had spent most of his adolescence in a center for those with special needs, but throughout, she had hoped he might go to a real high school one day. She knew it probably could never happen. His retardation is significant. Those with Down syndrome have one damaged chromosome; Andrew was born with three.

But three years ago Karen decided to try it. She arranged for him to go to the high school half days. That, however, only made him worse—the midday transitions were confusing—and they had to give up.

Then, two Septembers ago, the family learned that the school's special-needs teacher, a woman named Pat Collins, had gotten enough budget for an assistant. So they tried again, this time putting Andrew there full days.

It was difficult at first. Because he could not communicate well, he would sometimes show his frustration by acting out physically, throwing books. At lunch, around the other students, he would get too loud. Still, the special needs teacher persevered, though the price was that Andrew had to be kept isolated, restricted to his classroom, eating lunch just with a teacher.

In one way, that was all right with Karen. Her greatest concern was that someone as different as Andrew might be ridiculed by the other students. She knows how kids are at high school age. She doesn't even blame them, it's asking a lot of adolescents to show grace to an awkwardly handicapped person placed suddenly among them.

Still, Karen kept hold of a small hope: That in time, Andrew might join the other students in limited activities. She hoped that some students might acknowledge him, and support him. She even dreamed that some might befriend him. But she knew that was not realistic.

The Jeep Cherokee approached the school and parked. They got out the wheelchair and began to push Andrew toward the building.

He was her oldest child, and seemed fine when he was born, except for some trouble breathing at birth. Although slow as an infant, the doctors said he would catch up. Andrew's syndrome, called chromosome translocation, does not affect his features, as does Down syndrome, so there was no visual sign of abnormality. Don't worry, the doctors said.

But somewhere deep, Karen knew. She read all the books about what Andrew was supposed to be doing, like sitting up, and he wasn't. At last, at age 2, when he was not walking or talking, she and her husband checked him into the hospital for testing. She will never forget when the psychologist walked into the room as her son lay sleeping in a nearby crib. She knew the psychologist had been planning to do extensive IQ testing.

She asked him: "Are you done?"

"Yes."

"What are the results?"

"Well," the psychologist said, "on this particular test, he scored 55."

She knew about IQ scores. It sank in right away.

"Are you telling me my son is retarded," she said.

"Well," said the psychologist, "if you can believe the test, then yes."

After he left, she could only think the same things over and over: My son will never have a family, never go to college, never even go to high school.

But now, here they were.

Pat Collins, the special needs teacher, met the family in the lobby and took Andrew. The family went to their seats. Soon the moment approached; the chairwoman of the town school committee began the awarding of diplomas.

At last, it was Andrew's turn. Slowly, in his awkward step, he climbed the stairs onto the stage and began to limp toward the podium. Karen thought this would be a moment meaningful only to the family, and that was fine. She pointed her camera.

But then she began to hear it. Applause. It got louder and louder.

Onstage, Andrew stopped, stunned, and stared at his classmates.

Then something else happened. The 200 students of the graduating class began to stand, until every one of them was up. Then the 1,000 guests took the students' lead and stood, too. Andrew's eyes swept back and forth. From the sea of caps and gowns, he heard his named shouted out again and again.

Karen had known little about this. She had known that at last Andrew had begun to eat in the cafeteria, and go to art and gym. And when she walked into the school this day, she had seen how the other graduates approached him, and shook his hand, some of the girls kissing him, telling him that they would miss him.

But this applause, this standing ovation, the way it went on for a minute, and then two and even three—Karen had no idea the other students had been there for him this much.

At the podium, Andrew did not seem to know what to do. His teacher was waiting with his wheelchair on the other side of the stage, but you could tell she'd decided not to intervene. She just watched, wanting him to complete this moment without help. He did. He took his diploma. And as he at last came to his teacher offstage, and embraced her, she began to weep. He had done it. Andrew Singleton had graduated.

Now she began to wheel him back to his place, but it still wasn't over. The applause kept going, the people kept standing.

Somewhere among them, Karen Singleton applauded, too, proud of her son, but even prouder of these young men and women who found it in their hearts to stand by him.

DOWN QUILTS, FRESH-GROUND COFFEE AND GEESE IN A PERFECT V

Things That Make Life Worth Living:

■ Trench coats, white robes and crisp, thick pages in hardcover books.

■ Dustbusters, no-stick omelet pans and the sound of rawhide against wood in the spring.

■ Autotellers, pizzas delivered to your front door and being the first in a crowded supermarket to notice a newly opened register.

■ "Rainy Night in Georgia," Swiss Army knives and down quilts on cold nights.

■ Room service, Huckleberry Finn and hitting a triple word score in Scrabble.

■ Fleece gloves, ice cream cones with colored sprinkles and falling asleep to the sound of rain on the roof.

■ Warm croissants, blood-red leaves in October and having a whole afternoon in a bookstore.

■ Horses' noses, the smell of newly ground coffee in the morning and dogs who put their chin on your knee when you're feeling sad.

■ Heinz ketchup, shooting stars and geese flying overhead in a V.

■The zoo on a sunny day, catching snowflakes on your tongue and Christopher Plummer singing Edelweiss at the end of The Sound of Music.

■ Jean shirts, character breakfasts at Disney World and carry-out Chinese food in cardboard cartons in front of junk television.

■ Fat newspapers on Sunday mornings, hot showers at the end of cold days and down quilts.

■ Lamb chops, dogs that sleep on their backs and hammocks with pillows.

■ Mountain bikes with shock absorbers, college greens and a big yellow full moon just inches above the horizon.

■ Carousels in summer, the seek button on car radios and having the answering machine on when the phone rings during dinner.

■ Automatic ice makers, rolltop desks and eating a hot dog with a ball game in front of it.

■ TV remotes, foghorns in the distance and those hot washcloths handed out by flight attendants at the end of a long trip.

■ Cornbread, signed baseballs and having a choice of 20 ice cream mix- ins.

■ Movies with Robin Williams, movies with Jimmy Stewart and movies period.

■ Spring rolls, old streets with cobblestones and the way newborns squeeze your fingertip when you touch their palms.

■ Curbside check-in, covered bridges and seeing an osprey catch a fish.

■ The smell of new cars, "Summertime" by Janis Joplin and glass milk bottles waiting for you outside the door at 6 a.m.

■ Shrink-wrapped food baskets, bowling a strike and roasting wienies.

■ Toys in Happy Meals, 2-year-olds in bluejean overalls and a roaring blaze in a living-room fireplace come February.

■ Tub margarine, CNN Headline News and hotels that turn down your bed and leave chocolate on your pillow.

■ Picking apples, favorite books that are even better the second time and the way two-year-olds use creative English.

■ Dr. Seuss, snowman-making weather and rental movies that cost less than a coffee and muffin.

■ Itty-Bitty Book Lights, watches where the whole face glows in the dark and delivery people bearing big boxes.

■ Raucous political campaigns, horse-drawn carriage rides and seeing wild animals in the woods.

■ Dessert cafes, laptop computers and getting into bed at 8 p.m. with a pile of magazines.

■ New jogging shoes; better yet, old ones with no pressure points; better still, ski boots with no pressure points.

■ The morning paper on your doorstep, a second pillow at night and those little thumb-shaped crabs that dance on the edge of ocean waves and then disappear into the sand.

■ The mounted patrol, doctor's offices with current magazines and having the first suitcase to emerge onto the airport baggage carousel.

■ Jogging strollers—even if you don't jog, morning mist over a pond and the Jungle Ride at the Magic Kingdom.

■ Hawks overhead, getting onto a three-way row of plane seats with no one assigned next to you and ``good job" notes from bosses who seldom give them.

■ Climbable trees, personal mail and one of those songs coming on the radio that takes you way back.

■ Kites, ice-makers and the service department saying, ``No problem. That's on warranty."

■ Hand-held vacuums, 16 megabytes ram and those two weeks in spring when the drabbest shrubs are in full color.

■ Heated pools, shrimp cocktail and learning at O'Hare that your plane is at Gate 1 rather than 322, .

■ A parking space four steps from the restaurant door, microwave popcorn and lying on the grass staring up at the brightest stars you've ever seen.

■ Country inns, popovers and white terry cloth bath robes . . .

■ . . . Oreos, echoes and rainbows . . .

■ . . . and lastly, though not leastly, spacious skies, majestic mountains and waves of amber grain.

🕐

TO THOSE WHO PASSED THE TORCH

The stewardess said the flight would last 11 hours. At least I had a window seat. Maybe I'd even have the whole row to myself. But no luck. The plane was full, and an older couple ended up next to me.

As we climbed to altitude, I opened a book. It didn't work. The man began to talk to me. Where you from? Any kids? He told me they were retired—both in their 70s. He went on a bit about his career. To be polite, I asked him how he got started in it.

"Well," he said, "that goes back to the war."

At that, I made the mistake of saying it.

"You were in the war?"

Yes, he said, he was. He headed a tank division. "But I don't want to bore you with the stories."

Mistake number two: "No," I said. "Go ahead. Where were you stationed?"

Right away, I regretted saying it.

"Europe," he told me. And he began: About some of the battles, and how his tank unit beat Patton to the Rhine, but most people don't know about that. At least I think he said the Rhine. I wasn't paying a lot of attention. I'd been through this before—trapped by an older man telling me World War II stories. Still, I tried to be polite. "You take many casualties?" I asked.

Did they ever, he said. Only 40 of his unit—or maybe he said "division"—survived out of 120. At least I think those were the numbers. By now, I'd begun to flip through the airline magazine, eyeing the entertainment section. I hoped there would be a classic-rock channel for the earphones. You know, the Stones, Joni Mitchell. Those were the days, college days, younger days.

I began to think about those days: Growing up free. Growing up with a nice lawn, with Little League, with a secure world.

I may have protested America for a while, in my teens, but looking back, I had to admit: It was a great country, and still is. A free country. Prosperous, too; the Depression was my parents' world, not mine.

In high school, we danced to the Beatles, then I went off to college in Vermont, and I still joke that I spent as much time on ski slopes as in classes. Everyone likes to talk about how they came up the hard way, but in truth, most people my age had it pretty good. Pretty free.

And as I sat there on the plane, something suddenly occurred to me. There is a reason I had it so good, so free, and it's this: Older folks like the man sitting next to me sacrificed their own youth, for me.

At the same age I was dancing to the Beatles, worried mostly about girls, he was worried about basic training. At the age I was dodging college classes and sneaking off to ski, he was shipping out to Europe, saying goodbye to those he loved, unsure whether he would see them again.

At the age I was leaving college to hunt for a job in a job-rich market, he was leading a tank unit into Europe, postponing the start of his own career. At the age I'd begun working, still chasing girls, building my future, he was fighting the German army.

What would have happened if he'd lost? It's unsettling to ponder. But he didn't lose. Which is why I grew up in security, and prosperity, never thinking that those things came with a price, and that the price was paid by this older man sitting next to me, and millions like him.

I hope I'll think a little different about older men and their war stories from now on. Because the truth is this: Most of the things my generation holds dear, and takes for granted, in fact had to be battled for, and won, by soldiers like them. And if it's not too late to say it, let this story be my thanks.

🕑

I just saw what could be my favorite tabloid headline ever.

"Bigfoot Stole My Wife," it said.

Beneath, a sub-headline added detail: "Distraught Hubby Vows Vengeance on Beast That Took his Woman."

The story appeared in the Weekly World News. I figured it had to be true; newspapers always print the truth—ask any politician. Besides, names were included. It seems that James Larmore of Sanders, Fla. lost his wife to a "man-beast" who lured her into a back-to-nature love nest.

The story was written by William Dean. I wanted to get in on it. The World News is based in Lantana, Fla. I called.

"I'm sorry, sir," the News receptionist said. "If you want further information on any story, you'll have to send a request in writing."

I told her I was a reporter on deadline. I needed to talk to William Dean about his Bigfoot dispatch. She put me on hold for over a minute.

"Sir?" she finally said. "The Bigfoot story was done by a stringer who didn't leave any phone number or address."

I asked for the editor, but he wouldn't talk to me. I guess I don't blame him. Any good editor would try to keep a competitor away from his scoop.

I decided to play dirty. I called back in a disguised voice, insisting I had a news tip for the editor. The receptionist told me to wait. A little ingenuity, that's all it takes. Any second now, I'd get through. The receptionist came back on the line.

"Are you the reporter who just called here?" she asked.

"How did you know?"

"Sir, we just can't help you."

So. There was no choice now but to dig out the story on my own. I dialed the operator and asked the area code for Sanders, Fla.

"I don't show a Sanders, sir," she said. "But I do have a Sanderson."

That had to be it. A typo; happens all the time. Sanderson is seven miles below Georgia. It has no local police, but there's a sheriff's department in neighboring Macclenny. Kenneth Roberts, county jail supervisor, answered the phone.

This is not satire by the way; there is a real Kenneth Rogers who is truly the jail supervisor in Macclenny. I told him I was following up a Weekly World News story on a Sanderson man's wife carried off by Bigfoot.

"Never heard of that," Roberts said. "We got some bigfooted men around here, but nothin' like that."

I asked if he'd gotten reports on Bigfoot in the past. This is where I broke through. The trick to this business is asking the right questions.

"Not Bigfoot," he said, "but we got something called the Taylor Wild Man." He explained that Taylor is a wooded area north of Sanderson. Check a map if you don't believe me. "The young boys and all that talk about a big hairy man wearin' overalls," Roberts said, "this sort of thing. Steals chickens and this sort of thing."

I began to think. Maybe the Taylor Wild Man did it, not Bigfoot. And maybe Roberts didn't know about it because James Larmore hadn't reported it to the authorities. If he was bent on revenge, as the News said, he'd want to keep it to himself. I called directory assistance. Believe it not, they actually had a listing for a Jimmy Lauramore of Sanderson. The Weekly World News had reported a James Larmore in Sanders, Fla. It had to be the same person. I dialed the number. A man named Marty Sheffield answered his phone.

"Jimmy Lauramore?" he said. "He's my uncle."

I asked about Bigfoot.

Sheffield's word-for-word answer: "That's the first I heard of a Bigfoot, but there's a Taylor Wild Man. All I heard is he's a big old wild man out in the woods, but everybody said he's out there."

"What's he do?" I asked.

"Just roams the woods," Sheffield said. "Kills calves and hogs, stuff like that."

"Well," I said. "I have a newspaper story here that says a creature like the Taylor Wild Man carried off Jim Lauramore's wife."

"Norma Jean?" Sheffield said. "Not that I know of. He ain't told me nothing about it."

The story, I explained, said that Bigfoot and the wife had set up a love nest.

"Not Norma Jean," Sheffield said. "She's scared to death of the woods. I wouldn't know why anyone would want to say something about her running off with the Wild Man. That tickles. She'd probably flip she heard that. Jimmy's the only one she ever been with. Her daddy and mommy brought her up strict."

I did not make up that quote. I couldn't if I tried.

Still, if this particular Jim Lauramore was not involved, I was at a dead end.

Unless.

I tried one more hunch.

Did Sheffield know any other James Lauramores in the Sanderson area?

"James?" he said. "I got another uncle named James."

It was the final possibility. I asked: Was there any chance that this second James's wife ran off with the Taylor Wild Man?

"Cain't picture it," Sheffield said. "James got her pretty well trained. She does what he tells her. She stays home."

"Maybe Bigfoot took her against her will," I said.

"Cain't picture that, either," Sheffield said. "If the Wild Man wanted somethin' like that, shew. I couldn't imagine the wild man wanting that."

"No?"

"No. Lord, no," Sheffield replied. "There's better 'round here. If he came out the woods and saw her, he'd probably turn 'round and run back in."

Maybe that's what happened. And maybe James Lauramore's wife ran in after him. Maybe she even caught him. Maybe, when I nail this story down, I'll be able to flaunt a headline even better than the one in the World News.

"My Wife Stole Bigfoot."

A HARD WORKER SEES THE BIGGER PICTURE

The drive back home from the Lordstown plant was only 15 minutes, but he was almost too tired to face it. He'd been putting in six-day weeks for a month. At least now, midafternoon Saturday, it was over.

For the last 18 years, David Metzler had worked for General Motors, lately as a machine repairman in the stamping facility in Lordstown, Ohio. He had two daughters, a son and too many bills, which is why he welcomed the overtime, despite the Saturdays it cost him. Without it, his income would be in the 20s. The previous year, he was able to build it to $32,000. His wife worked part-time as a cook at the local middle school, bringing home $5,000. Together, they had enough for basics, but not much more, certainly not college bills. As Metzler drove home, that was on his mind.

College, he felt, was about the best thing he could do for his children. It frustrated him that he couldn't afford the most desired schools, but he had talked with them about that, and they'd done what they could to help. Metzler recalled the day his eldest daughter won the 3,000 meters at the Junior Olympics in Lincoln, Nebraska—best in the country. It earned her a full scholarship.

Now it was the turn of his boy, David Jr., 18 and an excellent wrestler. Metzler would have liked to have taken his son to more weekend matches, but he needed the overtime instead. His hope was for his son to make it to State, his best chance for scholarship money. Without it, there was no way the family could afford full tuition.

Once, Metzler had applied for tuition assistance, but it became clear there wasn't much hope. With income close to $40,000, he was in the middle; too high for aid, too low to afford it himself. He hoped he could find a way to make college possible for his boy. David was a good kid. All his children were. They didn't do dope, they pulled their own weight. His son earned dating money cutting firewood.

But this day, as Metzler drove home, he thought more about burdens than blessings.

His pickup truck was 16 years old with close to 100,000 miles. He hoped to keep it held together another four years, until his son graduated college. He also hoped there would be another vacation for him and his wife sometime. They'd taken a week in St. Lucia for their 25th a few years before, but it was the only such trip they had been able to afford in a decade.

He arrived home about 3 p.m., still beat. The hydraulic system of a big milling machine had broken down that morning, and fought him for hours before he'd gotten it fixed. He poured himself a cup of coffee and thumbed through some bills. There were some sizable ones, especially Visa. He had flown his youngest girl, a nurse, up from South Carolina for Christmas and helped his oldest, now a track coach at Youngstown U., fly down to New York for a teaching seminar at Columbia. The total was over $500. He began to wonder if he would ever get ahead.

He picked up the paper, glanced at sports, then began to leaf through the rest of it. That's when he came to an article that made him stop.

It was about working people who can't afford to eat. Specifically, it profiled a single mother with four children. She was too proud to go on welfare, so she'd taken a $4-an-hour job and was only able to feed her kids by picking up free groceries at the local church. Without that church, she said in the article, well, they'd be hungry.

Metzler put down the paper. Then he began to do some mental additions. After taxes, with time and a half, his pay that Saturday would come to $100. There was an address in the article for Second Harvest, the national organization that supplies food shelters. He took out a piece of lined paper and wrote out a letter.

"To Whom It May Concern," it began. "I came home from work at a GM auto factory bitching about all the overtime I've had to work lately. Kids in college—bills—etc. Then I read an article about your organization and the people you serve. I've quit complaining and you folks can have the hundred bucks I earned today. I hope it helps feed some kids. If it does, I helped myself, too."

Metzler mailed off the check quietly. He did not seek attention for what he did. But Second Harvest happened to send me his letter. When I called him, he was at first hesitant about publicity.

"I don't want you to think I'm some kind of saint," he said. "It's only $100. I see in the paper some organizations give thousands."

I pressed him on why he did it.

"I spend a lot of time in the factory fixing machines," he said. "Sometimes, I think I should be fixing people, too."

Before I said goodbye, I asked his plans for the future. It was a short answer. He hoped to cut down at the plant so he can take his boy to wrestling matches, he said. He wants to do all he can to give him a chance at college.

ALL I'VE LEARNED ABOUT HOW TO LIVE

I hope this doesn't disappoint Mr. Price, my college English professor, who spent years schooling me in James Joyce, but if given a test, I'd be far more adept at quoting Fulghum.

As in Robert. As in, "All I Really Need to Know I Learned in Kindergarten." That was an essay boiling down life's rules into a short list. I chanced upon it again recently. Among other things, it includes these:

■ Share everything.

■ Play fair.

■ Put things back where you found them.

Everyone doubtless has such a list in them, only as I sat down to try one myself, a problem occurred to me. Lists like this are probably best done in pencil. My own All-I-Really-Know-About-How-To-Live list would have been one thing at age 23 and quite different, even contradictory, today at 43.

So maybe the best approach would be to contrast them:

THEN: Rent, don't buy.

NOW: Buy, don't rent.

THEN: Keep your horizon at six months.

NOW: Sink roots.

THEN: Play the field.

NOW: Find a soulmate.

THEN: If your partner gets too needy, put wheels under him or her.

NOW: Hang onto each other hardest when your bond is being tested.

THEN: Push the edge.

NOW: Know your limitations.

THEN: Instant gratification takes too long.

NOW: Take your time.

THEN: Remember Bogart's line: "There's more to life than dames, like doing the right thing for a pal."

NOW: There's more to life than pals, like doing the right thing for a dame.

THEN: If you don't sweat, it's not a sport.

NOW: Take time to watch the birds.

THEN: Run like the wind.

NOW: Pace yourself.

THEN: Never eat dinner before 9.

NOW: Never eat dinner after 9.

THEN: The more the merrier.

NOW: Less is more.

THEN: Sleep late and seize the night.

NOW: Go to bed early and seize the dawn.

THEN: Tell your buddies about your exploits, particularly romantic.

NOW: You don't have to talk about it to feel you've done it.

THEN: Children? Freedom is richer.

NOW: Freedom? Children are richer.

A FACE I'LL REMEMBER

The news from Africa seems always of its dark side: Poverty, tribal wars, dictators.

But there is another side.

I was late for my plane.

I'd been in Ethiopia a week for my newspaper and was heading to the Sudan. If I missed this flight, there wouldn't be another for days. As I left the hotel, I zipped my most important item into a vest pocket: My leather billfold.

I'd spent a month planning this trip. Ethiopia was my first stop with five countries to go. If I lost that billfold, it would be over. First, there was the money—$10,000 in traveler's checks and cash. There was my elaborate plane ticket. Most important, there was my passport, stamped with six precious visas. I'd spent weeks begging for them, knocking on embassy doors in Washington, following up with dozens of international telexes and 2 a.m. phone calls—African governments don't easily admit journalists.

That billfold was my life. There would be zero chance of getting new visas. People I met in Addis Ababa told me often to hold onto that billfold tightly. For an average Ethiopian, it would mean three lifetimes of wealth. Day and even night I kept it zipped into the right pocket of a khaki vest I wore at all times.

In places of poverty, such as Ethiopia, airports draw hordes. The Addis airport this day was chaos. Dozens of people hovered around each arriving cab, offering to carry luggage. Inside, hundreds more went up to passengers offering any other kind of help.

The ticket line—there was only one—took an hour. When I got to the front, an agent shook his head. He pointed across the room to a crowd. Fill out a customs form and come back, he said. Now I began to panic. I hadn't planned on this delay. I forced my way through the crowd. People jostled me.

"Carry bags," said a voice, and another, and a third. No thanks, I said and pulled out a customs form. It asked for my passport and visa numbers.

I took out my billfold and laid it on the table, copying down the information. Time was moving fast. Behind me, a surge of people came through the main door and moved toward the ticket line. Quickly, I shoved back through the crowd to queue up before them.

Over the next 20 minutes, the line moved well. I was going to make this plane after all. I reached into my vest pocket for my ticket.

My billfold wasn't there.

I patted my other pockets. Nothing. I looked on the ground. No luck. Someone had picked my pocket. No, it was worse than that, it was me—I'd left the billfold at the customs table. I looked over there. All I saw was a mob of people.

It was over. I had set up dozens of appointments—in Sudan, Kenya, Burkina Faso, Mali—but all of that was over. At this compelling moment of trying to get news out about Africa's famine, I'd have to come home, embarrassed before my bosses, my colleagues, my newspaper's readers.

I threaded through the crowd toward the customs table. It was pointless, of course. I got close and saw the surface—no billfold. It was over.

That's when I saw him. I'll always remember his face. He was a tall African man with a white, floor-length native gown. He was perhaps 50, clearly not wealthy. He leaned on an elbow, sedately smoking a pipe, showing the most amused of smiles. I met his eyes, and then saw what he was holding aloft in his right hand. My billfold.

He arched a playful eyebrow, as if to scold me, then pressed the billfold in my hand and physically closed my fingers around it. I opened it up and everything was there. Instinctively, I took out a wad of cash—probably $100—and offered it to him. He smiled wider but shook his head. Not necessary. He simply pointed to the ticket line. Go catch your plane, young man.

I did.

And I'll never forget him.

Or that side of Africa.

L.A. WEEKEND

I spent the weekend in Los Angeles for a family wedding, just two days, but it was enough to confirm that what they say about it is true.

It began even before I left home, in the airport line, where the man behind me struck up a conversation, revealing he was an L.A. travel agent, but just to pay the bills; his real calling was author. I asked what he'd written. Nothing yet, he said.

Six hours later, we touched down.

At the baggage pickup, local women came in with expensive fashions on top and jeans on the bottom. The jean knees all had 4-inch razor sharp cuts. Some were parents meeting college students. In many cases, the only way to tell the mothers from the daughters was by looking at the corners of their eyes.

I was relieved to hear that my cab driver was not doing TV scripts on the side. He was, however, fasting. Ramadan, he explained. The traffic jam began five minutes out of the airport and ended five minutes from the hotel.

I took a stroll. The preferred fashion among men seemed to be black shirts, black pants, black ties and black sports jackets. Most rolled the jacket cuffs halfway to their elbows. None of the graying, older men had paunches. Most had tennis shoes.

Back in my hotel room, I opened a brochure listing exercise classes. One was called "Abs, glutes and thighs."

I met my brother, who told me he'd seen a homeless person wearing an animal rights button. Another held out a can and said: "United Homeless Pizza Fund." My brother gave.

That night, I came back late to find a crush of beautiful people—perhaps 1,000—leaving the hotel banquet hall. The women, all blond, had necklines to their navels and hemlines almost as high. The men, all in tuxedos, did not have haircuts but hairdos. I was convinced it was the pre-Oscar dinner; it was that elaborate. It turned out to be an awards banquet exclusively for sound editors. It was one of a half-dozen wannabe ceremonies around L.A. Oscar weekend.

The next day, I walked Rodeo Drive in Beverly Hills. People were checking their own reflections in store windows. Many mannequins wore jeans with razor cuts at the knees. I tried to go into a store called Bijan, but the doorman said I needed an appointment. Inside, it was empty.

I went jogging and saw a three-Mercedes house. I saw two other houses with landscaped driveways: Checkerboards of concrete squares separated by 3-inch wide grass strips manicured as finely as golf greens.

I opened the newspaper and spotted a story about a graduate school professor promising money back to any student dissatisfied with his teaching. Los Angeles magazine had a dozen pages of cosmetic surgery ads, including one for the Collagen Clinic, one for the Leg Center, one headlined "Recreate Your Ears," and one featuring a handsome surgeon asking, "Are you beginning to look like your mother?"

I ate at a few delis. The waiters who weren't screenwriters were weightlifters.

It became clear why houses in L.A. canyons fall down. If people are able to find or gouge a 1,000 square foot plateau on a cliff, they will build a 999-square-foot foundation. One house had a footprint bigger than the available land, if you include the backyard tennis court which was in midair, three-quarters of it sticking out like an enormous diving board held up by stilts. The neighborhood was called Mount Olympus.

I left Oscar morning. Starting at 6 a.m., TV stations began flashing urgent updates from the Shrine Auditorium. A crowd of onlookers were interviewed. They'd been camped there two nights—in the rain—so that when the time came, they could get a few 10 second glimpses of celebrities walking by.

I headed to the hotel elevator where a sign warned me to use the stairs, not in case of fire but earthquake.

Finally, on the plane, I knew at least I had material for a column. Though now I'm thinking: Maybe I should expand it to a screenplay.

That's what I really do on the side.   ⊕

He was awakened by something he hadn't heard in a long while: The absence of sound. He lay there for a time just listening to it, waiting for something to break it—an engine, a radio, a burglar alarm, something familiar, but there was nothing. All he could hear was an occasional faint sound that he finally identified as the creaking of pine trees. The breeze was so light, he couldn't even hear that; just a soft creaking. That's how quiet it was.

He and his wife had come for the weekend to this inn. It was an inn in the woods, on an island off the Atlantic coast. It had been hard for them to block in the time. Both could have used the weekend to catch up on things at their offices. But this was the inn where they'd been married. It was time to come back.

At first, he was disappointed that there was no television in the room. When he travels, it's the first thing he looks for. It's important, when you're on the road, to still be in touch, catching the news. He especially liked the kind of hotels that have TV controls at bedside. That way, you can go to sleep watching the late movie and in the morning, as the first act of the day, draw yourself awake by flipping channels. But there was no TV here. No radio, either. If he had remembered that, he'd have brought his own, along with a cassette player. He hadn't remembered.

That's why the silence woke him.

Usually, he is awakened by a clock radio. He sets it for 6 sharp, and after falling back asleep, is reawakened soon by other noise, urban noise; by traffic or garbage trucks or sirens. He doesn't consider most urban noise an annoyance. Noise is part of a city. You can grow as addicted to it as to coffee. Natural or not, it becomes part of you, and had long ago become part of him.

It's that way for him at work as well. He works as a newspaper columnist, and while writing, he no longer hears all the newsroom phones. Curiously, it's more distracting when they stop. It's hard for him to concentrate in a silent office. Outside, he finds a silent city just as unnerving. On summer weekends, when his neighborhood empties out, and the bustle beyond slows down, it sits strangely with him. He finds himself missing the sound of traffic. His world seems more natural with noise. Perhaps it's why he reads better with a TV on in the background. And why the first thing he does after starting his car is reach for the radio.

It's how he and his wife spent most of the 90 minute drive to the island ferry, flipping from station to station. He did the same thing while driving around the island their first morning there. But late in the day, they were passing a pond when he heard a strange song. He stopped the car and turned off the radio. It was like a thousand crickets, but truer and more melodic.

"Pinkletinks," his wife explained. She knew the island better than he. They're a kind of tree toad that live around ponds. She said their song is so much part of the culture here that the island newspaper runs a story each spring when the first pinkletink is heard.

That's when he stopped turning on the radio. That afternoon, they took a long walk on the beach. They heard geese honking. And gulls, and terns. It occurred to him that he could not remember the last time he'd paused to just listen to the world.

After the beach, back at the inn, he paused again, outside the car, and heard the ocean in a way he'd never heard it before. At first he thought it was the wind, because the ocean was more than a mile away, and was calm that day, almost no waves. But it wasn't the wind; he could tell because the trees were still. It was the sound of shifting water. He'd never realized that when you are in a coastal place with no cars, no breeze, no noise at all, you can actually hear a calm, distant ocean; you can hear the shifting of its surface.

Then came the next morning, when the silence startled him awake. When was the last time he'd heard silence? It reminded him of a page from Moby Dick, about how the smell of land can be as strange to the sailor as the smell of tide is to mainlanders. Stay at sea long enough, said Melville, and you stop noticing the salt air. It's land then that becomes foreign, and even before a sailor sees it, he smells it, a faint but distinct smell of earthiness and vegetation. The soul who never goes to sea will die without truly knowing the smell of continents, the smell of the world. They will miss that.

Just as those addicted to noise will miss something. Isak Dinesen wrote of it in Out of Africa. "Civilized people," she said, "have lost their aptitude of stillness, and must take lessons in silence from the wild."

By the time the weekend was over, he came to understand something about those lessons. They are not just about listening to the creaking of pines. They have more to do with clarity of the mind.

PORTRAIT OF THE ARTIST

I've spent the last few days reading a book describing how real writers do it. My favorite paragraph is on Hemingway:

"Nowhere is the dedication he gives his art more evident than in the bedroom where early in the morning Hemingway gets up to stand in absolute concentration in front of his reading board, perspiring heavily when the work is going well, miserable when the artistic touch momentarily vanishes, slave of a self-imposed discipline which lasts until about noon when he leaves for his daily half-mile swim."

I found that in the Paris Review writers' series, a group of books profiling authors. In the event they'd want to include me in their next volume, I give them, for free, this rundown:

Understanding a writer's need for self-discipline, Patinkin reaches from under the covers at 6 sharp and slaps his alarm clock onto the bedroom carpet. An hour later, he sits up suddenly, inspired by his 4-year-old asking if there will be breakfast before school today.

The true craftsman understands that the discipline of writing must be matched by a discipline in one's personal life. It is why he regiments his diet strictly, usually eating whatever is left behind on his children's plates. As he eats, he makes sure to read the back of all nearby cereal boxes, hoping he'll find something worth writing a column about.

By 8:45, the school-drop done, Patinkin is marshaling his creative forces. He does this by going to a neighborhood drug store to buy four newspapers, hoping he'll find something worth writing a column about.

He is usually the last to arrive in the downtown lot he uses, and can find no available spaces except the dark one beneath the expressway overpass, where he has involuntarily donated several car stereos to the needy. At first, this didn't bother him, as the true artist views even personal crises as material. But there is a rule in journalism that says you can't write more than two columns about having your tape deck stolen, and Patinkin has already written three.

A soldier for routine, Patinkin makes sure to stop at Dunkin Donuts on his way to his office, where he buys a regular with colored sprinkles. He then buys six magazines at a nearby newsstand. He reads through five of them in search of columns. With the sixth, he just looks at the pictures.

No artist comes to maturity without a beacon to learn from. Patinkin, too, has been a great student of the techniques of others, particularly Hemingway's edict that one should never talk about writing, as it depletes the creative well. Patinkin practices a variation on this around colleagues by heading off potential questions about his own work with the following inquiry: "Got any column ideas?"

Just as an artist needs beacons during his coming of age, so too, he needs mentors when he's in the full flower of his productivity. Patinkin works alongside editors who give him just this kind of salutary guidance. Often they will place character-building notes in his mailbox, saying such things as, "You call that a column?" Or, "You expect us to print this?"

By noon, Patinkin is still waiting for his creative reservoir to fill, a process he usually seeks to enhance by going to lunch. Two hours later, after returning to his desk by way of Dunkin Donuts, he is sensing the peaking of his literary energy. This, now, is the artist's telltale moment, the time of looking into his own soul. It takes beyond-human effort to focus all thoughts on this one task: The forming of the article's first sentence. Slowly, Patinkin reaches his typing hand forward. For a moment, it hovers over the keys.

Then he pushes the "store" button and queue-switches over to the Associated Press wire so he can scroll through the day's dispatches, looking for something to write a column about. He does this for an hour.

At this point, we come to the hinge on which literature turns. Patinkin's editor will walk up and tell him he has 60 minutes to deadline. With a look of hurt in his eyes, Patinkin will explain that an artist must work from inspiration, not desperation.

Invariably, the editor will listen patiently while lighting his pipe. He will then look up and say, "You now have 59 minutes."

Within seconds, as if by magic, the lead sentence appears. The prose now builds in momentum, as Patinkin seemingly hears audible voices urging him forth, voices that say things like, "You now have 34 minutes."

Finally, his work completed, Patinkin returns home and lives true to the discipline of his personal life, eating whatever is left on his children's plates for dinner.

When asked about his secret, Patinkin merely shrugs and says that art is a mystical thing. He then sets his alarm for 6, lies down in bed, picks up the remote, puts on earphones so his wife won't get angry, and spends the next hour surfing repeatedly through 59 channels, praying the basic prayer of the journalistic artist before passing out.

That he'll find something worth writing a column about.

🕐

SIMPLE THINGS

It had been five years since I'd done anything like this. You approach 40 and you come to appreciate comforts. Camping in the mountains begins to seem more burden than escape.

Then, a few weeks ago, a brother of mine said he was planning a trip. It'll be great, he said: A 10-mile hike to a natural hot spring 12,000 feet high, nestled at the top of a valley in Colorado. Come on, he said. Don't be so middle-aged. Let's do it.

I flew west, and we started the next morning at 9. We took off at a fast pace, then got realistic and slowed, finally stopping after five miles for lunch. That's when I learned what the world's best food is: Any food after you've been hiking uphill for three hours in high altitude with 35 pounds on your back. We shared some dry, stale bagels. They were terrific.

We hiked a few hours more. To our left, a crystal stream roared by; but even in the Rocky Mountain wilderness, there are parasites you're supposed to be careful of, so we had to go slow on the water we'd packed. Now, though, I was parched. I poured canteen water into a tin cup and stirred in a spoonful of Tang powder. I noticed several gnats floating on the surface and a half-dozen specks of dirt. The Tang was weak. The water was warm.

I couldn't remember the last time a drink tasted so good.

Back to the trail, higher and harder, the sun soon sinking and the air cooling. At last, we made it. We set down our gear. Now that we'd stopped, my wet shirt began freezing in the cold wind. Quickly, we set up the tent and walked 50 yards to the hot spring. The last few miles, I'd daydreamed myself into fantasies of a landscaped spa with attendants and clean white towels.

The spring turned out to be a muddy pool about 3 feet deep and 10 feet long. There were rocks on the bottom, and some scummy seaweed at the sides. It was difficult to get into a comfortable position for long.

And no Jacuzzi ever felt this good.

By 7, we were famished. We pulled on our dirty jeans and went back to the campsite. For dinner, my brother had brought something that looked awful—freeze-dried chicken Tetrazzini. He undercooked it, leaving the rice hard enough to crunch. I poured a serving into a dirty tin plate, dipped dry bagels in it and washed it down with weak Tang.

It was the best dinner I'd had all year.

Soon, there in the high mountain wind, we began to get cold again. At 8, we went back down to the spring. A couple joined us just after. They'd come in over the pass from Crested Butte. He built houses; she was a waitress. A few others followed, including a woman from New Bedford, Mass., who'd lost her sales job in a bad economy and had come west looking for a new life.

We lingered well into the night, everyone soaking for hours, no one uncomfortable when silences fell; that was part of what we'd come looking for. I'd never realized there were so many stars up there.

Just before 11, the moon helped us find the tent again, but we didn't last long. It's hard to sleep in a tent, especially one staked on angled ground. By 5 a.m., we were back in the spring—same seaweed, same rocky bottom, same muddy water.

And I haven't known a better morning bath before or since.

At 6:45, the sun hit the top of the peaks. Slowly, the light crawled down the mountains, hitting the pool about 9:30. That gave us the courage to get out.

We headed back about 10, and by 11:30, we'd finished our water. The sun was hot, and as the hours went by, I got thirstier and thirstier. I tried to lick my lips, but even my tongue was dry. Finally, midafternoon, we made it to the car and sped five miles to a roadside food stand. I got an extra-large cup filled with ice, then mixed in imported seltzer water and gourmet cranberry juice. A perfect spritzer. I drank it down nonstop.

Somehow, it wasn't as quenching as the warm Tang.

There was a Jacuzzi where we were staying. It had a plastic bench contoured for perfect comfort, the jets adjustable for just the right massage, the water crystal clear.

It felt nowhere near as nice as the muddy hot spring.

By the time I was on the plane the next morning, the soreness had set in. My legs ached, and so did my feet. I was exhausted from lack of sleep. My lips were still felt parched and sunburned. I thought back to tossing all night in a cold tent on rock-hard ground. It occurred to me that I hadn't been through such a physically uncomfortable few days in some time.

But I got something back for the price, a reminder of a value forgotten.

Simple things...

🕐

I'LL KEEP MY PRIDE ON THIS TEST IF IT KILLS ME

I **just figured out** why Americans die young.

We lie on health forms.

I had to fill one out recently and found that a strange thing happens when you have to put down personal data. It doesn't matter that it's for a doctor; you still portray yourself as you want to be, not as you are.

Take the first question: It asked whether I was big-boned, small-boned or average. All males, even accountants, want to be big-boned. It makes us feel like Arnold. That's why I buy extra-large shirts when medium would probably do. I did the same thing here. The honest answer would be "average." I put down big-boned.

The next question was height. I'm 5-feet-10—actually 10-and-a-half; males always add a half inch. Still, this has long bothered me since men hate being under 6 feet, especially around women with heels. Now, on my health form, I had my chance to compensate. I marked the "6 feet" box. Close enough.

Then we got into the guilt section.

"Do you eat four servings of fruits and vegetables," it asked, "four servings of breads, grains and cereals, two servings of milk products and two of meat, fish or plant protein? Daily? Thrice weekly? Or seldom?"

You read something like that and right away it all goes back to the mother thing, to the time you were 9, and Mom walked up to you with the crystal dish you broke that morning, and said, "Mark Alan Patinkin, are you responsible for this?" Mothers always use your middle name when they're mad.

Anyway, I told her I'd never seen the dish before.

The same impulse made me check "daily" for balanced meals. I'm not about to tell a doctor I eat Nestle's Crunch and Pepsi for lunch. I was afraid I'd be scolded unless I denied guilt. Plus, it was clear what the right answer was, and I wanted to score high.

This raises another problem with health forms: The questions are too accusatory. "Do you limit your intake of cholesterol?" it asked next. "Of salt, of saturated fats, of sugar?"

Who's going to admit they don't? Besides, a question like that isn't about your dietary habits. What it really asks is this: "Are you weak and self-destructive? Yes or no?"

I checked the appropriate box. Of course I limit my intake of all those things. What broken crystal dish?

I moved to the exercise section. Do I do at least 20 minutes of vigorous conditioning daily? Or three times a week? Or seldom?

In other words: "Are you in shape? Or a sloth?"

I put down "daily."

I once read an essay by another columnist who took a similar test, the kind where you have to tally your answers. The score will then tell you how many more years you have to live. The columnist said he added it up and discovered he died four years before. He mentioned this to a colleague.

"Now that you mention it," the colleague said, "you have been looking a little pale lately."

Ever since, I've been especially wary of these tests. There are things I don't want to know. Nothing will make you die young quicker than the stress of knowing you're about to die young.

The next question was about car safety. Did I wear my seat belt always? Sometimes? Or never? If ever there was a case of entrapment, this was it. Leaving off your seat belt is a crime in some states. If I was in the business of robbing drug stores and a written test asked me whether I rob drugstores, my answer would be obvious.

Broken crystal dish? Never seen it before.

Yes, I said, I always wear my seat belt.

You see this same dynamic around ticket counters for commuter airlines. If the plane is small enough, the agent asks each passenger their weight. I was once sitting close enough to watch the responses. The women who were over 150 all insisted they were 125. One day, one of those planes is going to go down, but at least the women aboard will have their self-esteem.

It'll be the same with me. I'll be lying in a hospital, felled by cholesterol-induced blockages, but at least I'll be able to tell myself I'm big-boned and 6-feet tall.

I finished the test. The results said I was mediocre, which I think is unfair, because the main reason was a family history of heart disease. I don't see why I should be penalized just because I had relatives with health problems.

I also got a danger flag on my immunization record. The questionnaire had asked for a listing of shots I'd had in the past 10 years. Who keeps track of shots? I put down the honest answer—"Don't know." And what happens? I get a danger warning.

I've learned my lesson. Next time, I insist I've got full immunizations. And I leave out the health problems of my past relatives. I didn't know them that well, anyway.

I can't wait for my next medical test. Now that I know the right answers, I should get an impressive score. I may even put down that I'm 6-2; I've always wanted to be that tall.

THE SAINT

At **first, this didn't seem** the kind of story I'd be interested in. It had to do with a stained-glass window in a church, and, well, theology is for the religion page. I'm not the kind of writer who is comfortable starting the word "He" in capitals, at least in the middle of a sentence. I haven't thought much about what God is, let alone written about it.

But I found myself driving to the church to see this window, because it seemed to say something about how we live, or should.

The basics are this: A church needed renovation but didn't have the money; it got the job done anyway because some tradesmen volunteered their extra time for four years. As gratitude, the parishioners used the face of the head carpenter for St. Joseph on a stained-glass window.

Normally, it's the kind of story I would have passed along. Not my thing. But something about it got me thinking, so here I was, at St. Catherine Church, on the common of a scenic New England hamlet called Little Compton.

Here's how little I know about religion: I had to ask the priest who St. Joseph was.

He was polite. "The husband of Mary," he said.

"Of course."

Then he told me how the window happened: Joseph was a carpenter, no one really knows what he looked like, so why not use the face of Edward Souza, the carpenter who donated the most time to the renovation?

I had to talk Souza into meeting me at the church. He doesn't like a fuss. You think of saints and you picture majesty; Edward Souza doesn't fit that. He wore beat-up boots and an old, gray work uniform with flecks of white paint on the pants. He's 60 years old, drives a 1987 Oldsmobile with 140,000 miles and went no further than high school. When I asked about hobbies, he said he had none, except for spending time with family.

Before the renovation, the church was a converted meeting hall with frosted windows. "All I could think of was a locker room whenever I walked in," the pastor told me.

So the congregation's 470 families raised $330,000 to overhaul it. It wasn't enough. That's when Souza and five other tradesmen said they'd help. After their day jobs, they began to work several nights a week, 6 to 9 p.m. They kept at it for four years. When it was over, the building committee came up with a novel way to show its gratitude: Put Souza's face in one of the new windows.

On my way out, I paused to look at it. The words beneath it said, "Saint Joseph The Carpenter." It showed Joseph leaning over a workbench in a biblical-era carpentry shop. The face, clearly, is Souza's, he of the beat-up boots and Oldsmobile with 140,000 miles on it.

End of story.

At first, I still wasn't sure I'd write about it. Like I said, I'm not into religion. But as I drove home, I got to thinking.

If God is anything, at least in this modern time, he's not a being, but a force. I don't see an Oz-like figure above, pulling levers. If anyone pulls levers, we do.

We decide whether to be good or evil, to look away or not when someone needs help. We decide whether to give our time and sweat not for money, but simply because a thing is worthy. You want to see what God looks like? Don't wait for Him—here I go with the upper case H's—to reveal Himself as Charlton Heston with a flowing beard. You ask me, the way He shows himself is in the good works of common folk.

Like, say, the folks who spend days stacking sandbags to save the homes of strangers from floods. And just maybe, like what happened at St. Catherine.

But let's get even deeper now. Let's get to Edward Souza. There he is, pictured as a saint. He's not one of course, he'd be the first to insist, but perhaps his being there can make a difference. Because there is this problem with true saints. They are god-like. People kneel before their images. Almost none of us can aspire to be that pure.

But we can aspire to this unlikely face on the wall of this church: A simple soul with paint flecks on his pants who did a thing few of us do but more of us could: Gave dearly of his time for no payback except that a thing seemed worthy.

There's a small postscript to this story. When Edward Souza saw the window, his reaction was to ask the church to change it. He was almost embarrassed. He didn't think he deserved it. He still doesn't. He told me so. After all, he said, there were five other guys.

MY NEXT THRILLER

A **suspense writer named Ken Follett** just got $12 million from
Dell Publishing for his next two books. Another suspense writer,
Jeffrey Archer, made a three-book deal with HarperCollins for $20 million.
Newspapers do not pay this much. So I'm switching professions. If Dell
and HarperCollins are out there, what follows is the first installment of my
next thriller:

As I adjusted my taupe cravat and poured myself a Courvoisier XO
from my 19th-century cut glass decanter, my office door suddenly opened.
I recognized the face. Good old Sarbanes. Choate, '56, now head of the
Secret Service; White House detail. His face looked like 50 miles of bad
road.

"The President's Manhattan motorcade leaves in one hour," he said.
"And intelligence tells us Gadhafi has paid Carlos to take him out."

"Relax. The French arrested Carlos a year ago. Don't you read?"

"He escaped last week. Interpol is keeping it quiet."

So. Carlos. The Jackal. Achille Lauro, '85. For decades he'd eluded the
CIA, and even Israel's Mossad. Now he was going after the Old Man.

"Please," begged Sarbanes. "We're out of leads." His aide,
Bartholomew, whom I never trusted—the man even looks like a weasel—
was at his side.

I downed my XO. "Where's the President's limo?" I asked.

"Outside," said Sarbanes. "It's clean."

"I wouldn't trust you clowns to clean my decanter," I said and popped
the hood. After reaching behind the carburetor, I stood straight. "You're
right. Clean. It'll obviously be an outside hit. I'll take the job."

In the office, the door opened again. The sight of her knocked the wind
out of me. Hermione. Hermione of that month in Paris. Hermione who left
me to marry money—and now wants both. Her nostrils were flaring. "Take
me," she said. I have a lot of bad habits, but married women isn't one of
them.

"Next time," I said, "bring a note from your husband."

Outside, I climbed into my '64 Ferrari 250 GTL Lusso. A half-hour later, I was in Mohammed's penthouse. For years, he'd fed me the beef on terrorism. In return, I'd let him keep his cute little arms-smuggling racket. But that was over. I grabbed him by the shirt, including some skin to drive home my point.

"The feds might be real interested in those Kalashnikovs you snuck through the Port last week," I said.

"But I've played ball for years."

"That was yesterday, pond scum. This is today. Either I get the line on Carlos or you eat breakfast at Rikers."

"All I know is it's an inside job. Guy named Bartholomew at the Secret Service. I got a number for his cell phone, secure line. Call him, disguise your voice, tell him the code word is Tripoli. Ask where Jackal is."

So. It was a mole. And the mole was The Weasel. I made the call. I got an address—Office 3838, 43rd and Fifth. I was there in minutes, just as the motorcade rounded the corner below. I kicked open the door. Carlos was inside. "You got a search warrant?" he said.

"I keep it in my $835 Cole-Hahn crocodile Barlettas," I said.

Then a shock. He pulled Hermione from a shadow and used her as a shield.

"I'll kill her," said Carlos. "And you'll never save the President anyway. He's 40 feet from a mine that'll detonate in five seconds."

I drew my .359 Magnum. The barrel spat hot metal and tore a briefcase- sized hunk of brisket out of Carlos's exposed side. He fell dead. "Sayonara," I said.

Then I reached into my pocket and pushed a button. Thirty-eight stories below, Limo One screeched to a halt. Eight feet in front of it, the asphalt erupted in a shower of hellfire. A moment later, I was standing with Sarbanes.

"How'd you stop the car?" he asked.

"That day I checked the limo," I said, "I planted a remote control stop on the brakes. Somebody had to take care of the Old Man."

Then I pointed at The Weasel. "There's the key to your case," I said. Bartholomew cursed me. I told him to save it for the judge.

Suddenly, Hermione ran to me. "I've left my husband," she said. "I've left everything. For you."

"Sorry, kid," I said. "I've already got a spouse. My work."

She wept.

I walked away into the fog.

Alone.

If Dell and HarperCollins want more chapters, I'm not greedy. An even $5 million will be fine.

🕐

SOLO FLIGHT

My seat was toward the front of the plane. As I settled in, an unlikely passenger appeared. She was a little girl, no older than 4, alone except for a stewardess helping her into the empty row across from me. She was blond and wore a blue jumper with a red shirt underneath. The stewardess got her something to draw with, and a snack.

I couldn't recall seeing a child that young traveling solo on a plane before, but she seemed fine about it, as if she'd been through this a few times.

The stewardess soon stopped by my own seat. Her name tag said Jeannette. I asked about the girl.

She'd just had a visitation with her father in the midwest, Jeannette explained; now she was coming back east.

I said she seemed young to be traveling alone.

Jeannette smiled. Airline rules say children have to be at least 5 to ride unaccompanied, and the parents have to sign a paper attesting to that. But the little girl had just told the stewardess she was 4. It happens that way a lot, Jeannette said.

A part of me understood: Plane tickets cost money, and if you don't have much, and are divorced, and paying support, you have to cut corners to stay in touch with your children. And the Midwest father seemed responsible enough. Before putting his little girl on the plane, Jeannette said, he'd cautioned her to be careful about talking with strangers. That's how the girl ended up being brought to the empty row across from me— she'd at first been in a cramped row and had appeared nervous about it.

"She's fine now," said Jeannette. "She's a good traveler."

I asked if she had this kind of passenger often.

"All the time," said Jeannette. In the last few years, it had become especially common. During summers, peak visitation time, planes often have kids like this.

She stressed that the airline takes thorough precautions. Many papers have to be signed, and the person picking up the child needs elaborate identification.

Throughout the flight, I kept sneaking glances at the little girl as she worked on little drawings.

I tried to understand. I told myself this kind of thing is unavoidable, just as divorce is. Often, divorce is best for the adults involved, just as following a new spouse or job across country is best for them. Who is anyone else to judge?

But then I couldn't help it. I couldn't help but wonder if sometimes, we're losing track of what's best for children.

The plane touched down. Jeanette asked the little girl if she was looking forward to seeing her mother at the airport.

"My dad's picking me up."

"Oh," said Jeannette, the smile still there, "I thought you said you just visited your dad."

"I did. I have two dads."

The little girl took another stewardess's hand and walked in front of me down the jet-way. Inside the terminal, she spotted a man and ran up to him.

The stewardess took out the paperwork. The ID's checked out. The package was delivered.

🕐

I knew this would be a gamble. We'd gotten theater tickets in Boston and decided to splurge on a fancy restaurant. I've always been wary of fancy restaurants. You never know if you'll end up with one that's so fancy they'll serve minuscule portions. I don't know why, but the posher restaurants think it's a sign of distinction to serve as your entree a 3-ounce crayfish with four string beans projecting from its snout like whiskers. Nothing else on the plate. For $28. Salad, $10 extra.

If need be, I suppose I can handle small portions, as long as I can at least order a steak and a potato. My deepest fear is of restaurants that are so chic they only offer food you've never heard of.

That was the gamble. I opened the menu. Gamble lost.

I barely recognized a thing on the menu, though it was in English. Those items I vaguely recognized I wished I hadn't.

Begin with the sub-categories. I looked for "Salads." I did not see it mentioned anywhere. What I saw was "Legumia." What is Legumia?

Then I looked for Appetizers. It wasn't there, either. But I did see a category called Offal. What is Offal?

Finally, though, I saw "Meat." I liked that. Better even than Entrees. "Meat" is unpretentious. I presumed the items beneath it would be as simple, so I searched for a steak. I didn't find it. The first listing was "Agnolotti of marrow and preserved cabbage with crisp shreds of beef." Pass.

Next: "Tamarind smoked pork ribs and winter cabbage slaw." Quickly, I moved on to "Sudado: shortribs of beef with cumin seed and cilantro." I liked the shortribs part, but was wary of the cumin seed and cilantro, so I dropped down to the last choice. Please be a steak. It wasn't. "Roast loin of rabbit with rabbit chile," it said. Couldn't they at least have covered it with normal chile?

I took heart at the next category. "Fish." Blessedly, the first listing at last looked recognizable: "Chilled Maine oysters and Cape Cod clams." I'd found my entree. Not so fast. I kept reading. "With salad of fresh cut seaweed." Said seaweed was a $10.50 add-on to the package. For that kind of money, couldn't they have used real lettuce?

Maybe they'd let me substitute, so I switched back to Legumina on the guess that Legumia means greens. There had to be a normal salad in here. There it was: "Salad of crisp greens and soft white beans." Normally, I'm not a big soft-white-beans-on-my-salad type, but I'd put up with them. It was the best alternative. Then I kept reading: ". . . over transparent salt cod." I will eat a salad with apples if I must, with walnuts, cucumbers and 10 other ingredients. I will not, however, eat a salad on transparent salt cod, which I've never heard of.

I kept scanning Legumina. Had to be a real salad in here somewhere. What I found instead was "curried skewered onions charred in Tandoori oven." There was also "chestnuts roasted and buttered, with song sung by Warren," which I almost took, then decided I'd be embarrassed to have some chef named Warren singing at my table while I ate my chestnuts.

I was getting desperate now. It left me no choice but to wander into the mysterious category of Offal. It didn't look promising. "Mondongo," announced one listing, adding: "uncommon tripe soup with plantain and avocado." I was in the mood for soup, but couldn't risk it. At a place like this, Mondongo could easily end up being calves' brains.

Then I spotted the item following it. Calves' brains.

Specifically: "Calves' brains with crisp fried capers and sherry vinegar." This, too, was an appetizer. Great way to get you in the mood for the main course.

I asked the waiter if this listing was the owner's idea of humor. He glared at me with the same revulsion I'd shown toward the menu and explained that calves' brains happen to be a favorite among many regulars.

You mean people come back?

Two days later, I'm still trying to recover. I see only one way to get over it. I'm going to a Bonanza Steakhouse. Sirloin strip, please, medium well, hold the agnolotti. And waiter, when you bring my salad, seaweed on the side.

MARION

I met her in the desert of Africa. I was there to write about hunger. She was UNICEF's representative for Timbuktu.

And now I am on vacation in Aspen and I just read that an Air Mali flight out of that city had crashed. It took several days for Reuters to file a dispatch listing the names. I finally saw it in the New York Times. Marion vanDensen was among the dead.

She was fluent in several languages. She could navigate a Land-Rover through desert dunes. She had short blond hair. She was 29.

Two days before Christmas, I flew up from Bamako, the capital, to see her work. She met me at the airport. I did not expect to find such a woman in such a place.

Timbuktu is harsh country now, dying country. There are things young Western women are supposed to love. Those things are all around me here in Aspen. There was none of it in Timbuktu. It is mostly a place of hardship. And desert. It was difficult for me to understand what drew her.

It is also difficult for me to understand why her death is affecting me so much. I knew her only a few days. But as I ride the chairlifts, I find myself thinking only of her. Perhaps it is because the contrast speaks of what she was about. To tell you about Marion vanDensen, I must first tell you about Aspen.

I love this town. I especially love the people. They are as cheerful as any I have known. They are also intelligent. I had a cab driver who mentioned that he was an architect. Aspen is full of that kind of thing, professionals who tend bar because living here is what's important.

But among many, you notice there is something missing. The talk seems to be only of the next slope, the next drink, the next good time. Perhaps there's nothing wrong with that. In the end, we are most of us in quest of ease, and I'm as guilty as anyone. That's why I came here to play.

Still, the contrast is one reason I am so affected by the news about Marion. It is hard to find people like her these days. It is hard to find people who search not for ease, but for a way to give something back.

She was sent to Timbuktu with a simple call. People are starving, UNICEF said. Children are starving. Her job was to find them and keep them from dying.

As I remember, she wore old T-shirts and jeans. We spent 10 hours driving through the desert one day, stalling on dunes, bouncing over furrows. Camels walked by. After a few hours, I was ready to go back. She insisted we keep going. She wanted me to see. She wanted people to know what was happening to the nomads of Timbuktu.

I remember a few moments.

We drove by a group of five women. Marion noticed one was bent over a sick child. She told the driver to stop. Then she knelt and spent 15 minutes looking the child over. In a few days, she would come back to this encampment with medication.

A few hours later, we were about to board a boat to cross an arm of the Niger. I'd read that the river is full of parasites: Schistosomiasis. I kept my shoes on and leaped aboard. Marion laughed, rolled up her trouser legs and waded in.

"Don't be so paranoid," she said.

The most enthusiastic I saw her was toward the end of the day, in a village called Ber. We walked to a parched field outside it. In its center, there stood a solitary pipe. UNICEF had sunk it for irrigation. Emergency food was one thing, said Marion, but this pipe was special. She told me to touch it; she told me it was hope.

I remember how exhausted I was on the way back to the city. It was night. The desert is a place without landmarks. It will swallow you if you don't know it. Our driver delivered us by the stars.

Marion sat in the front with an elder from Ber who'd asked for a ride. While I half-dozed, the two talked the whole way back, laughing much of the time, this young Dutch woman and this old Mali nomad. It is one of the things she taught me: That you can't wait for the world to bring you your joy; it's on you to draw it from whatever's nearby.

She taught me some other lessons. One of the more lasting comes back to Aspen. There seems to be a thread that runs through some of the women here. Like the men, they come looking for good times, but beneath it, they are also looking for something else, something like rescue. In subtler forms I see that in many women back in the world: the search for a life raft. Marion had gotten beyond that. There are no life rafts in Timbuktu, but she went anyway.

For a while, I wondered how this could be enough for her. How could desert and work be enough? What about escape? What about ease? What about the search for a life's partner?

I was having lunch at a lodge on one of the ski slopes this week when a possible answer came to me. Always in Aspen, there is a rush to catch the new powder, the best nightspots. It is not just the college types, but the older ones, too, maybe especially them. There seems to be an urgency to having a good time here, a fast time, maybe because deep down, people know it's all gaining on them.

Marion didn't have that. I guess when you've found something that's for the world, you don't have to work as hard to chase good times for yourself. And perhaps she found another secret, too: That fulfillment—even joy—comes not just from play, but from taking on hard things.

There is one image I will always remember about her. Her yard. She lived in a house surrounded by sand, but the sand was giving way to green: She'd planted trees. They were just seedlings when I saw them, maybe six inches high, but I knew she'd make them grow. It is a good measure of a life—whether you can blossom in a place of harshness. She did. And she left a good legacy, too. She gave a few things back.

So let us say a prayer for this woman. And perhaps, to honor what she stood for, let us make some gesture to help her work go forth.

THIS I BELIEVE

I believe in the way babies wake every morning with a smile, in the public's right not to know and that military wives who have babies alone while their husbands are overseas should get medals.

I believe that golf should be reclassified as an addiction, that they don't make men like Gary Cooper anymore and that the surest way to lose a spouse's devotion is to presume it a given.

I believe that if you focus on stardom first, craftsmanship second, you'll never be a star, that both men and women should have at least one job in their lives that builds calluses on their palms and that peaking young is a curse.

I believe that employees work harder for bosses they like than those they fear, that Slim Jims should be on the EPA Superfund list and that sometimes there's nothing better than a rainy day on vacation.

I believe you should never hire someone with a bumper sticker saying TGIF, that the salaries of both CEOs and baseball players should be tied to their year-end statistics and that grudges weigh too much to lug around half your life.

I believe that the cruelest thing a journalist can do to some politicians is quote them accurately, that God's way of making separation with children easier was to invent adolescence and that it would break the hearts of Babe Ruth, Lou Gehrig and Ty Cobb if they ever found out about AstroTurf.

I believe that when a doctor says this may be just a tad uncomfortable you'd better ask for morphine, that when a pilot says the repair will take five minutes he really means an hour and that you can tell someone's character by how they treat salespeople,

I believe that men would be happier if they made a point of not shaving one day a week, that yippy lap dogs should be categorized as members of the rodent family and that there's no such things as quality time with kids, just time.

I believe that J.D. Salinger owes it to those of us who were changed by Catcher In The Rye to write another book, that too many people marry the wrong person because they don't want to be impolite and that whoever wrote the mouthwash commercial featuring people saying, "You can kiss me now" should be sentenced to watch a week of Mr. Whipple ads.

I believe in sitting in a beach chair just at the lip of where the waves wash up, that when your wife asks whether she's gained weight it's best to fib and that anyone who tells you boys and girls are made different by society rather than biology hasn't had one of each.

I believe that deep down, mothers like to worry, that parents who see their young girls climbing trees should say "how brave" rather than "be careful," and that if you spend a week in Africa or even Germany, you'll never take the American phone system for granted again.

I believe that women with a few lines on their faces are more interesting than cute young cookies, that the stock market is a casino and that any man over 50 who dates a girl under 25 should be required to get a note of permission from her mother.

And finally, one more.

I believe that if you're a parent, no matter what profession you go into—no matter how ambitiously you work at it—you'll never be able to judge whether you're a true success.

...until your children are grown.

🕐

THE VALUE OF BEING ENCUMBERED

It was late, past 8:30, the time I was supposed to have her home to bed, but it had been months since I'd had her alone for the night, and there was one more stop I wanted to make.

I lifted her out of the car seat and headed up the stairs, past the oversize ice cream cone in the window. Because of the hour, the other customers were all adults, mostly students.

I got a cone for each of us, then headed toward the booths in the back. That's when I saw I had company. There was another little girl, about the same age as my own, between 2 and 3. Briefly, I wondered why a mother would allow so small a child to stay out so late. Then I saw. As with me, the girl was alone with her dad.

In one sense, he wasn't the likeliest looking dad. There's something about becoming a father that tidies a man up, more so than marriage does. This father was wearing an old T-shirt and jeans. But he had father written all over him. Single men can be awkward around children, especially little girls. This guy seemed at ease. The look on his face said there was nothing he'd rather be doing.

I took the next booth. Right away, our daughters stood up and studied each other across the seatbacks, almost nose to nose. Then I caught the father's eye.

"My date," he said.

At the counter, more student couples came in, giggling nervously and trying to make a good impression on each other.

"Got one of my own," I said.

"Couldn't ask for a better date," he said.

Agreed.

He nodded. "They love you for who you are."

Then he focused back on his daughter, helping her with a drink of water, wiping off her mouth. Soon, across the seatbacks, the two little girls were touching each other and talking, as much as kids this age talk.

"We got a lot to learn from them," the man said.

I nodded. "They do get pretty comfortable around strangers."

"I know. No walls."

Then I asked if he had any other children.

"Just this one." I was surprised by what he said next. "Actually, she's not really mine. She lives upstairs with her mother. But the father's not around, so I kind of do that role."

He asked the little girl if she wanted sprinkles, then got up to get some. He told me he was a policeman. I asked where the father was. He made a dismissive gesture with his hand.

"Never see him," he said. "He doesn't come around. Doesn't care."

Any contact with him at all?

He made the same dismissive gesture. "He's got an order, but he's never paid a thing." He pointed to the little girl. "Her mother does it alone."

I asked if having one parent was tough on the child. "Hard to say. But I'll say this: I told her I'd take her out for ice cream a few days ago. Been working a lot since then and haven't seen her. Saw her tonight, and the first thing she said—instantly—'You promised to take me for ice cream.' So here we are."

"You don't mind?" I asked. "I mean, it's not like she's your own."

When he answered, he looked at her, not me. "Couldn't ask for a better date."

This is not meant to say that most divorced fathers are absent, or negligent. But some are, focusing mostly on chasing a new, unencumbered life.

They don't understand something this unlikely surrogate father did. There is reward in being encumbered.

I stood up just as a group of good-looking young women walked into the parlor. The policeman glanced at them, but barely noticed. As I headed onto the sidewalk, back toward my car, he was lingering there in the booth talking to his little girl.   🕐

JUDGED BY MY BETTER

One of the few advantages of being a journalist is you can't be replaced by computer. Software might be able to analyze data, but not craft prose. I was mentioning this to the newsroom computer specialist.

"At least computers can't write," I said.

"Yes they can," he said.

I asked what he was talking about.

He disappeared into his office, then came back with a software package called Rightwriter, made by a firm called Rightsoft. I took out the disk and looked it over.

"What's it do?"

"It'll edit your stories and tell you what's wrong with them."

I told him it sounded impossible. His response was to put the disk into the A-drive and ask for a recent story I'd written. I gave him the file name of my last column; he told the program to look it over.

The disk drive turned, the screen flashed a phrase. "Rightwriter is now analyzing the sentence structure."

Then the program announced it would be inserting comments into my text to tell me where my writing could be improved. It would also warn me if I was using too many adjectives or too much jargon.

"Jeez," I said, "eventually they're going to be able to get rid of people like me."

The computer specialist didn't smile. "Not eventually. Very soon."

Finally, the disk drive stopped. It told me I could call the story onscreen and see what was wrong with it. I did as I was told.

It began by giving the readability index—the grade level an average reader would need to understand my story. The number was 4.04. That meant just over fourth-grade level.

The computer specialist shook his head. "You're in worse shape than I thought."

I asked what the norm was. He showed me the Rightwriter manual. "Good business writing," it said, "ranges between 6th- and 10th-grade level." And I was 4.04.

The next number was writing strength. The optimum was 0.8. Mine came out just over 0.6. The computer guy asked: "You ever consider another line of work?"

Now came the real test. I began to look through the body of the story for comments. There were a lot of them. "Passive voice," the computer scolded. "Long sentence," it said at another point. "Repeated word," it told me. "Complex sentence," it scolded again.

"They can't talk to me like that," I said.

The computer specialist stared at the screen. He pointed out a few more comments. "Not a complete sentence," said one. "Unnecessary comma," said another. In every case, it was right. Still, I was a bit insulted.

"What gives them the right to judge me like this?" I asked.

"Well," the computer specialist said, "there's still time for a career in life insurance."

I ran another story of mine through the program. This one was a bit better, but not much—4.64 grade level. Again, I scrolled through for comments. Again, the computer was right every time.

It zeroed in on one phrase where I described a family as being straight out of Father Knows Best. The computer followed it by asking: "Is this explained?" It was right; I'll bet a lot of young readers would have had no idea what I was talking about. But how did the computer know enough to ask that?

Then it singled out this sentence: "I measured it with only one ruler: what I myself got out of it." The computer told me I'd used the wrong pronoun. "Replace 'I myself' by 'I' " it said.

Now I know how the human crew-members in "2001" felt about HAL.

Next, I got to an even more disturbing comment. It called one of my sentences "weak." Then it called another one "weak."

"What do they mean by weak?" I said.

The computer specialist felt sorry enough for me at this point not to answer.

Finally, the program gave me some general advice: "Consider using more predicate verbs," it said. I will. As soon as I find out what they are.

As a final test, I put this very column through Rightwriter.

It told me this was written at a 4.34 grade level. Then it told me to replace the word "optimum," which appears in the middle of the article, with the word "best." It also called me "weak" twice, and advised I put a comma after the word "eventually," which appears a third of the way down, in the paragraph beginning with "Jeez."

I began to think of HAL again. Remember the plot? Eventually, (note the comma), HAL got so smart he began to judge humans, then decided they were unworthy and tried to eliminate them.

Well, this computer wasn't going to get the best of me. I was smarter than it. Shrewder. That's the magic of the human mind. If we marshal our optimum brain power, we can come up with a complex, creative solution to outwit any machine. And staring triumphantly at the computer, I did. I turned it off.

🕐

A SCAR STILL TENDER

He awoke at his usual time, 5:45, before his wife and 4-year-old. He sat on his deck to read the morning paper. He spotted a column about Vietnam that drew him in. It was by a writer who had not been there, who'd avoided it through college, but confessed now that he felt shame for allowing others who weren't as privileged to fight and die in his place.

Chris is 38 and a plumber. The column got him thinking, and he decided to call the writer about it, but that would have to come later; he had a busy morning of putting in a new bathroom for a client. The job was worth $5,000, and he wished he were that lucky every week. He ran his own business, handed to him by his father, who taught him. He liked the work. No one told him when to jump.

He set down the newspaper and went upstairs to take a shower. Afterward, he stood in front of the sink to shave. The article was still on his mind; it had taken him back. In the mirror, he looked at his chest and saw the scar, just below his heart. It was about 2 inches long. It had begun as a bullet hole that got infected by the time they'd choppered him back from the field and opened him up.

He touched the scar again, and now he remembered.

It happened in 1972, in the jungle, though he doesn't call it jungle. That makes it sound too alien. He calls it the woods. It was 2 a.m. He'd been put on special forces, his job to go out at night to neutralize members of the Vietcong, who by day blended in as villagers. It was part of what made that war so difficult, Chris thought; you never knew who was on your side.

He was with a team of three, all wearing black clothes, their faces painted black. Each had a half-dozen knives strapped on, and several handguns. No rifle though; that made it too hard to run. The assignment was made easier for Chris because of what he'd seen done to others in his unit. Years later, he would remember a friend they had killed, and how they mutilated the body, and where the knife was left. It's what drove many GIs in Vietnam, Chris would explain, not the cause, but seeing what happened to your mates. The war became personal.

There in the dark woods, the three of them passed a hamlet. What happened next was very sudden. There was a sharp sound of gunfire, which surprised him; intelligence had said there weren't unfriendlies here. He and the other two began to run. There were more sharp bursts and then Chris felt his chest hit a branch, only it wasn't a branch.

He heard one of his buddies talk: "Stay down, stay down. You're bleeding, man." The bullet had struck him near the heart. The three of them lay there, trying not to move. If they got up to run, they'd be hit. All they could do was wait, and hope.

The gunfire stopped, but they knew to stay until light in case the enemy was waiting nearby to make sure. His buddies were named Willie and Michael. Willie was a black man, strong and over 6 feet.

Chris whispered: "I'm dying."

"Cut the crap," said Willie. "You ain't dying. You got to go home."

Willie took his own sock off and pressed it against the hole in Chris's chest. Soon, the sock was soaked, so Willie took off his T-shirt, tore it into strips, and compressed those against the hole, one after the other. An hour went by, then another and a third.

"You ain't dying," he kept saying. "Hang. Hang. Hang, man. Stay with me. Don't leave us alone."

Chris thought: What a place to die. Then he began to cry, though not for himself. He pictured his father picking up the box at the airplane. Years later, he wonders if that's what made him hold on: He didn't want to make his father meet a box.

Then morning came up. When it did, the three realized the hamlet was empty. It had probably been a stopping point for an enemy squad who heard noise, fired and moved on. Soon, they made it to a meeting place and were helicoptered out, and Chris found he'd been lucky, the bullet had passed through him without hitting artery, bone or organ.

Months later, after he recovered and went back to the war, the two were in another firefight. This time, Willie was struck. He was not able to hold on. "Talk to my momma," was the last thing he said.

There in the bathroom, Chris touched his scar again. Then he realized it was getting late. He spent the morning on the bathroom work, which did not go as quickly as he hoped. At lunch, he paused to call the columnist he'd read that morning.

All Chris meant to do was give a compliment, but the columnist kept him on the phone, drawing out memories. When their talk was almost over, Chris said he'd rather not have his name used. He didn't call to get publicity, he explained. He said he was no different from others like him who go through each day with baggage from the war, and few people understand because few really ask.

Then he apologized and said he had to go. He still had the bathtub to put in and was behind schedule.

🕐

A dozen pairs of white athletic socks, please."

What kind, sir?

"Like I said, white athletic socks."

Forgive me, sir, that's an outdated request. There's no such thing as white athletic socks anymore.

"There aren't?"

You have to be sport-specific, sir.

"Oh. Whatever. Running, biking, tennis, maybe baseball and walking."

Delighted, sir. How many pair for each sport?

"Each? You have different socks for different sports?"

Welcome to the '90s, sir. The difference is enormous. A running sock, for example, is designed with high-density padding under both the ball and heel of the foot to absorb impact.

"You're telling me I can't use that for biking, too?"

Out of the question, sir. A biking sock has ultra-thin construction and 50 percent Coolmax fiber.

"Coolmax?"

A four-channel fiber that helps transport moisture to the air.

"Tell you what, forget biking. My wife's been pressuring me to take an aerobics class. I'll just use the running socks for that."

You're joking, sir.

"Pardon?"

You can't wear running socks at an aerobics class.

"I can't?"

Of course not. The aerobic sock heel has a medium- rather than high-density construction because you're usually on your toes. Not to mention

Spandex over the arch to give you support while you're twisting in place, as opposed to running, which is forward motion.

"To be honest, I doubt I'll do aerobics after all. Maybe a little basketball. I'll just use my running socks for that."

A recipe for disaster, sir.

"It is?"

Absolutely. If you're going to play basketball, you need a sock with an extended heel pad to protect your Achilles' from being chafed by high-top shoes. Running socks don't have that. Do you plan on other sports?

"Maybe tennis. You're going to tell me there's a separate tennis sock?"

Night-and-day difference from the others, sir. For tennis, you must have not just high-density padding for sudden starts and stops, but stretch nylon over the toes to keep it from bunching up and causing blisters.

"Tell you what. If I promise to only use my running socks for jogging and walking, will you let me buy just the one model?"

Not in good conscience, sir. Walking is lower impact, so you need a medium- rather than high-density padding.

"What if I buy just tennis socks—could I use those for racquetball, too? It's almost the same sport."

You know better than that, sir. Racquetball socks are medium density in toe and heel, not high. And they include a special lace cushion.

"Okay, I give in. I'll buy two pair each for running, biking, basketball, walking, racquetball and tennis."

Very good, sir. Now as for height.

"Height?"

Height. Crew? Mini crew? Micro mini crew? Or rolltop?

"What's the difference?"

Each is a different altitude, sir. Selection of proper altitude is all-important in sport-specific socks. What'll it be?

"You know, I just realized something. I think I'm too old for sports."⬥

AMERICA'S MIRACLE

On the Russian countryside, once again, it is the time of another agricultural disaster. This year, rains blessed the land and the crop was bountiful, but there are not enough tractors to harvest, not enough freight cars to ship, not enough mills to process. Some would say there is also not enough initiative, a legacy of too many years of farming by central committee. And so, millions of tons of produce have begun to rot on the ground while store shelves are half-stocked.

Which brings up Jason Peckham.

He is part of an American miracle we seldom pause to honor. He is one of the nation's 2 million farmers, and on this morning, he was out with the sun, steering a tractor through part of his 375 acres of potatoes.

There is no committee to tell Jason Peckham when to harvest. He is an entrepreneur, part of a legion of them—farmers, truckers, millers, distributors. Together, unseen by most, they annually achieve one of the world's productive wonders.

It is an extraordinary thing to see a combine work. As big as a small garage, costing $100,000 and more, thousands move each year through the Midwest's wheat fields, the sickle shearing off the plant, the auger forcing it into the feeding house, the rotor thrashing off the seed while a fan blows out the chaff. In the great wheat farms, when the time is critical, six combines will run side by side, 24 hours a day, so that the kernels can be captured at their peak. The machines will stop only to be oiled and fueled.

The great shipping trucks seldom stop either. From the farms, they carry the wheat to enormous depots that hold up to 50 million bushels. From there, by train and barge, it is transported to the giant food companies, the General Mills's, the excess routed to elevator complexes in Galveston and Corpus Christi for shipment to a hungry world.

All the while, other combines gather the nation's oats and barley and corn, harvested in amounts that no other nation can match—250 million tons and more.

The milk we drink, the meat we eat, it comes not from a corporate monolith but independent farmers, many of them small, 50 cows, 100 cows, 200. Each morning, and again each evening, the ritual of milking is repeated, the udders sterilized, the milking machines attached, the stainless steel tanks filled in each barn, then emptied as trucks carrying 4,500 gallon haul the yield to the nation's thousand processing plants.

By year's end, America's farmers will have produced—and just as importantly shipped—150 billion pounds of milk, enough to fill a lake. They'll have shipped 25 billion pounds of beef and 18 billion pounds each of chicken and pork. They'll have gathered 60 million tons of wheat. They'll have moved almost all of it from farm to shelf in days or even hours.

On the farm of Jason Peckham, the morning harvest was soon back from the field, and into a grader that sifted out the culls before washing and bagging the potatoes themselves. By noon, he'd filled his refrigerated Mack truck with 4,000 10-pound bags, 20 tons of produce. The truck took off for Boston, and within four hours, potatoes that had that morning been in the rich loamy soil near Rhode Island's Atlantic shore, were on shelves waiting to be bought by consumers.

It did not mean his work was done. Far from it. Only minutes after the truck was gone, Peckham was again operating his Dahlman harvester. Soon, he'd brought from the ground 25 tons more, that, too, shipped as produce before dusk of the same day.

And across the land, on 2 million other farms, the rhythm of harvest and transport was similar.

A routine day's work, America's miracle.

🕐

LAURA WHO?

E**very so often,** you run into a moment that reminds you how old you're getting. I walked into a record shop and approached a clerk. He seemed young, but I'm young, too, which made us compatriots. I asked where I could find some Laura Nyro albums.

He gave me a blank stare. "What kind of music does she do?" he asked.

I figured he hadn't heard me.

"Laura Nyro," I repeated, more slowly.

Same blank stare.

Laura Nyro, I said again: Famous female vocalist, mid-to-late '60s. Everyone knows Laura Nyro.

His stare went from blank to pitying. "I'm sorry," he said, and didn't complete the sentence, but I know what he was thinking: "Sir, I wasn't born in the mid to late 1960s. I've never heard of this woman. I go to a dentist, not a periodontist. I eat dinner at 9, not 5:30 p.m. I'm young; you're old. Who is Laura Nyro?"

"Kind of folk rock," I said sheepishly.

He pointed to an aisle. I wandered toward it, feeling like I'd just asked where they keep the Perry Como 45s.

Forty-fives, by the way, are small vinyl records with one song on each side they used to make a long time ago.

This wasn't supposed to happen to people my age. I was born in 1953, center of the baby boom. You know the baby boom: Destined to forever be America's youth culture. This is what's happening to our culture instead: I walked into an elevator the other day expecting to hear homogenized Lawrence Welk. I didn't. The speakers were piping in a bland version of the Beatles. You know your time is past when they're playing your music on elevators.

Nor can I fix this by changing my taste since the philosophy of baby boom people is there's been no decent music since 1972. This grates somewhat on my wife, who is four years younger. "My babysitter used to listen to that," she says whenever I put on a CD.

Not long ago, I was in a drugstore and noticed a rack of "classic" rock tapes. By "classic," of course, they mean "great," not "old." Anyway, I picked up a cassette of hits from 1969. Then I went to the counter. Two female cashiers were there. They seemed young, but I'm young, too, which made us compatriots.

As they rang me up, I told them my wife would likely chew me out for bringing home more of her baby sitter's music. I figured I'd get a sympathetic laugh: The cashiers and I were youth culture co-conspirators.

Instead, blank stares.

"What I mean," I said, "is she's four years younger and only knew this stuff through her sitter."

More blank stares. Which finally prompted me to ask the two young women: "How old were you in 1969?"

They paused a beat and looked at each other.

"Sir," one of the girls finally said. "I wasn't born in 1969."

"Me neither, sir."

It may sound silly to be unnerved by that, but we're different than, say, people our parents' age. Most of them began having kids in their early 20s, so in their 40s, it was natural to view twenty-somethings as the next generation. But people like me delayed childbirth. I'm 43 and have a 2-year-old. I'm not supposed to be old enough to be the father of college grads. Only I am. Which means there's a whole generation now grown who views much of my music the way I used to view the big bands.

I'd like to know who I see about that.

I'm picturing now what happened to that record store clerk after work. He probably went out with some other twenty-something friends, first to an espresso cafe to hang out until 9 p.m., then dinner followed by clubbing at midnight. His friends probably asked how his day went.

"Routine," he said. "Except at one point an older guy came in and asked for a singer named Laura Nyro."

Blank stares all around. "Who's Laura Nyro?"

"Beats me. The old guy said she was big, but we don't even stock her. He looked so shocked he left without buttoning his coat. Hope he doesn't catch cold. That can be dangerous at that age."

🕐

THE UNAPPLAUDED CALLING

I just saw another remembrance of Jacqueline Kennedy Onassis, and like those I've read before, it missed her greatest legacy. Most articles about her mention the same four or five things: She elevated the arts, personified grace and taste, she restored the White House and fought to preserve architectural treasures; she gave America strength after the assassination and was an accomplished book editor.

But I'd offer a different legacy if I had to pick just one.

She was a good mother.

My bet is she herself was proudest of that. She often said as much. She was perhaps the most famous woman in the world, a national icon, achievements most would feel significant, but she saw it differently.

"If you bungle raising your children," she said, "nothing else much matters in life."

Most would say they agree, it's the correct sounding priority: "Nothing's more important to me than family." But those are easy words. In truth, we're in an age when full-time mothering is almost a scorned calling.

Too harsh? Talk to those who've chosen it. They will tell you how often they are made to feel underemployed, even inadequate. At gatherings, they get anxious if they are talking to someone new who asks them what they do.

"Raising children."

"Oh. That's wonderful." Translation: "That's it?" And soon, many will start looking over the mother's shoulder for someone more interesting, someone with a career who's actually doing something.

At times, working women can show the greatest scorn. A notable successor of Jackie's spoke of how she could have stayed home and baked; Implication: I'm better than that. A prominent television newswoman, asked if it's hard to be away from her daughter, said she didn't think the child would be psychologically scarred because she's not there to feed her ginger ale.

Forgive me, ladies, but there's a little more to it than that.

Any mother will tell you their work is complex and draining. Also, uncelebrated. There is no applause for the thousand little things an at-home mother does each day to shape decent human beings. The pressure never stops, especially the pressure they put on themselves to structure stimulating days for children who often resist. I've heard more than a few working women say: "I couldn't stay at home. It would drive me nuts." They are right. It does. Ask an at-home mother the last time she read the newspaper on the morning it was published.

The truth is, full-time motherhood is seldom chosen by women who lack ambition to work outside the home, it's chosen by those who would like to have careers, but feel this is where they're needed most.

I came across a quote from Helen Keller the other day which captured well the work of mothers. "I long to accomplish a great and noble task," she said, "but it is my chief duty to accomplish small tasks as if they were great and noble."

Just because those small tasks don't include doing law briefs or TV interviews is no reason to see them as something less.

All those years, people wondered: What's Jackie's life been like inside that well-screened, secluded world of hers? What's she been doing?

Raising her children, that's what.

And despite difficult odds, she didn't bungle it.

I can't imagine a better legacy.

LET THEM EAT MEATLOAF

The Arizona prison system has come up with what they openly admit is a harsh way to reprimand misbehaving inmates. It has nothing to do with solitary confinement, hard labor or the rack.

They feed them meatloaf.

Break jailhouse rules for five straight days and they make you eat it for a week. Many people found this amusing. As a former single male, I was insulted.

During that phase of my life, I survived on meatloaf. Since it was the fanciest dish I could make by myself, I even I considered it a delicacy. It is difficult to now hear that in the eyes of Arizona, my chosen diet amounted to punishment.

I called John Turner, the Arizona prison spokesman, to ask what you have to do to get put on meatloaf.

"We only use it in our maximum security cell block where our most incorrigible inmates are kept," he said.

That made me feel terrific. After college graduation, I was a single male for 13 years, which is how long I regularly ate meatloaf. Measuring by that, I would have qualified as Arizona's single most punished inmate.

The worst part of this story was the prisoners' reaction. They complained. They even started behaving better. Anything but meatloaf. They didn't want to be treated like animals.

So much for my once proud image of how I lived when single. It reminded me of the time burglars cleaned out my house but left my stereo turntable behind. It wasn't good enough for them. Living with that was bad enough. Now I find my lifestyle of 13 years was not only beneath the taste of active criminals, but imprisoned convicts, too.

Personally, I thought I did pretty well back then. Once a week, I washed my own underwear. Once a month, I changed my own sheets. Twice a year, I vacuumed. In 1984, I even washed out the bathtub.

My mother used to tell me to get women I was dating to do these things for me, but she didn't understand something; modern women aren't like her. Many aren't any better at vacuuming than we males, and the few women who did know how to do it held it back for barter.

"Marry me and possibly we'll negotiate about it," they said.

So it was all up to us. The washing, the vacuuming, and of course, the cooking.

Lacking culinary genes, single males fall back on a simple philosophy: The easier the dish, the likelier we are to cook it. Meatloaf was easy.

Here was my recipe, the only dish I still know how to do since I did it so often: You take some ground beef. Toss in bread crumbs. You pour on a pint of ketchup. Squish in an egg—holds it together. You form it into a brick. Bake for 40 minutes at 350 and you're good for a week. A big brick, two weeks.

That's why meatloaf was superior to chicken or steak. You could make it last. If I had a big brick of it, night after night, I'd open the refrigerator, tear off a handful, drop it on a plate, squeeze on some ketchup and finish dinner in 46 seconds.

The great thing about meatloaf is that you can eat it even if you cook it wrong. Once, by mistake, I baked it for an hour and a half at 400. No problem. I used a screw driver instead of a knife, chipped through the crust, chewed each bite for an extra 10 minutes and it went down fine. The only thing I had to be careful of was dropping it on my foot.

Then there was the time I undercooked it. Or did something wrong. I'd shaped a perfect loaf—four inches high, five wide and eight long. I couldn't find my meatloaf pan, so I put it on a cookie sheet. It came out an inch high and 12-by-12. It didn't bother me. I ate it with a spoon.

I don't know what the future holds for the Arizona meatloaf punishment program. The ACLU may sue. They called it cruel and unusual, which was perhaps the worst insult of all to those of us who ate it by choice rather than force.

Being married, I'm now mostly out of the cooking business. At first, I tried to hold up my end, but after sampling the early results, my wife revoked my oven privileges.

But I will say this. Had I known about the Arizona meatloaf punishment early in my single years, I would have changed my household menu. In the end, a self-respecting citizen can't settle for regular dinners that aren't even worthy of death row. In the name of dignity, I would have changed from eating basic unadorned meatloaf.

I would have cooked it with bacon on top.

TRUE LOVE

I'd resisted McDonald's at first, but now it is almost a weekly habit, because most restaurants are hard with children, and this one is easy, and in the end, that is what we all want parenting to be: carefree.

We found a seat by the window, and no, I kept saying, no more fries until you eat another bite of hamburger, but I didn't push it because I wanted this to be carefree, and then, in the corner, I saw them.

There was a middle-aged couple sitting on either side of a girl whose age I could not tell. She was perhaps 18, perhaps 25, perhaps more. It was obvious something was wrong with her. She wore a cushioned of neck brace, and every few moments would snap her head violently to the side. She seemed out of touch with her surroundings.

Patiently, the woman held up a hamburger. After a few moments, the girl focused on it and took a bite. The couple gave her encouragement for that, dabbing at the corners of her mouth with a napkin. Then the girl leaned back hard against the booth and snapped her head violently.

I caught the older woman's eye, and asked how she was doing.

"Oh," she said, sharing the smile, "the best we can."

"Your granddaughter?" I asked.

They both laughed at that. "Oh no," the woman said. "Our daughter. We're older parents, I guess."

"Makes two of us," I said, trying to recover.

I put my attention back to my own table, but it was hard. The girl kept snapping her head, ramming backward at times. I asked myself: Would I be able to do this? With such a child, would I have the resolve to venture into the world? It would be so much easier to have a meal at home. What gave them the strength to overcome that?

They fed her more, and each successful bite gave both parents a glow. Their daughter seemed unable to talk, but she did respond to their feeding her, and that was communication, and it gave them a glow.

Soon my own daughter and I were finished. Before I left, I decided to talk to the couple, in part out of curiosity, but there was another part too. Something told me I was seeing something extraordinary, something other than the girl's behavior, and I wanted to understand what it was.

The parents were gracious. It was a form of retardation, they explained and emotional difficulties as well. She tends to be very self-abusive, they said. The mother pointed to her daughter's arms; for the first time, I saw they were restrained with special bindings. Some days, said the mother, are better than others. She smiled and said this was a bad day.

Their daughter, they said, is in a special hospital now, but they take her on weekends, and occasional outings like this.

"It must be hard."

The mother smiled again. She seemed at peace with it. "You handle what you have to."

I told them goodbye, and as I began to leave I thought of the dreams all parents have: Athlete and scholar and marriage and grandchildren. I thought of those dreams. And I thought of how easy we all want parenting to be, and in truth, how it is indeed easy most of the time. Then I thought of how hard this must be, and how tempting to just let go, visit the institution a few times a year and move on with life.

But these parents don't do that, or want to. Nor do they hide in their home. If an excursion like this enhances their daughter's life even the smallest bit, it is worth it.

And I know now what I saw at that table. It can be described in a single word. It's a word we use often, and when we do, we usually picture perfection—a kiss at the altar, or a child's embrace. But from now on, when I think of this word, I will picture this couple, at that corner table in McDonald's, patiently feeding their daughter, because it is one of the purest forms of love I have seen.

⟨I⟩

I CAN LIVE WITHOUT A LOT, BUT NOT HEINZ

I think it's time people stopped beating up on Anthony O'Reilly. He's a corporate CEO who not long ago became a symbol of the overpaid executive. In a recent year, he took home $75.1 million.

For what was he paid? Making automobiles? Airplanes? Computers? Not exactly. What Anthony O'Reilly got $75.1 million for was making ketchup. He's the chairman of H.J. Heinz.

I suppose you could call his salary outrageous. You could ask why we pay our CEOs 10 times what they pay in Japan. And why O'Reilly—whose company is only 79th on the Fortune 500 list—should make more than CEOs who employ 10 times the people and create 10 times the profit. You could ask such questions.

But I say the man deserves it.

Let me explain by comparing. Another big money maker was Charles Lazarus, who took in $60 million for running Toys 'R' Us. I'm sure he did a fine job, but I don't need Toys 'R' Us. You can buy toys lots of places. Then there was Fred Smith—$51 million for running Federal Express. I like Federal Express—fabulous road staff—but plenty of folks deliver overnight. Head of Chrysler? A package worth $20 million, and I admit I like my Jeep, but there are other good cars out there.

As an exercise, I went through the United States' biggest 78 companies and decided I could live without just about all their products. IBM? There are other computers. Exxon? There's other gasoline. Kodak? Other film.

But as God is my witness, there is only one Heinz ketchup.

What's the worst that could happen if General Motors went under? Perhaps a disastrous ripple effect that would trigger recession. Not great, but we'd get through it.

The worst that could happen if Heinz went under?

There are no substitutes.

I would not survive it.

I put Heinz on everything: filet mignon, chicken, veal, brisket. I dip toast in it, and even pasta. If a waitress serves me an omelet without Heinz I just wait, even as it gets cold, until I get her to bring me a bottle.

One Valentine's Day, I took my wife to a very fancy restaurant called the White Horse Tavern. I ordered lamb chops in the $30 range and asked for Heinz. The waiter was so mortified he brought it in a nondescript little white dish. Camouflage. I heard that when word got back to the kitchen, they had to wrestle a hara-kiri knife from the chef's hands. That's his problem. I want what I want.

And don't you dare try to sneak me Hunts, which is catsup, not ketchup, and the major problem with Disney World as I see it; all they serve there is Hunts.

That last paragraph will probably get me a livid phone call from the ad executive at my newspaper who handles the Hunts account, but I have to live in truth.

Another truth: In my 43 years, I've never had a bad meal. The reason i that even if I hate something, I soak it in Heinz and don't know the difference. Where would that leave me if Heinz went under permanently? Probably in a long-term-care facility on heavy sedation for the rest of my life. If Anthony O'Reilly demands $85 million this year, I say pay him.

I hope no one takes this as making light of a serious problem in executive compensation. When General Motors pays its head guy $3 million for losing the company $4 billion, there's something wrong in America. When factory wages continue to decline while CEO salaries triple, something's wrong in America. It's time to put hard rules on this. Rule one: Tie salary to performance. Rule two: Pay huge stock options only if the stock performs over 5 or 10 years. Rule three: Lower a hard ceiling, even the best CEO should get no more than $5 or $10 million.

But then there's rule four: If they make something I can't live without, don't care what you pay them.

Which brings up Coca-Cola chairman Roberto Goizueta, who actually may eclipse O'Reilly with a package of $86 million. The truth is, I can't eat lunch without a Coke. Pepsi won't quite do. I need a Coke with my turkey sandwich. Coke Classic.

So do me a favor. If you want to go after someone, pick on that greedy Stephen Wolf, who made $18 million at United Airlines, or that grabby Craig McCaw of McCaw cellular, who once drew $53 million.

But hands off Roberto Goizueta.

And especially Tony O'Reilly, God bless the man.

They make what I need.

A WAY TO FACE THE HARD THINGS

I **had not talked** with her in a year.

"If you're busy, I can call back," she said.

"Christine." I said. "It's been a while."

"Really," she said. "I don't want to interrupt your day."

"It's good to hear your voice."

I was single at the time. We'd gone out a few years before, when we'd both just begun working. It was as serious as those things get when you're young, which means not very, but at the time, we thought it was.

Usually, with me anyway, when something like that ends, it ends. I was never good at staying friendly with ex's. Christine was one of few I stayed close with.

She lived in Albany. Her husband was a doctor. She had two children. We talked for a while about that. I told her she seems to leave me further behind every year. I added: "I still can't believe you didn't wait for me."

Her answer was a two word sentence. "Oh, Patinkin"—her shorthand for telling me I was full of it. Then she said there was a reason she was calling.

"I've got to have another biopsy."

We'd been together a few months when she told me there was a swelling on her neck that wouldn't go away. Weeks before, her doctor had said it was probably from flu, but swollen glands should have gone down by then. She arranged to go in for tests.

I'll always remember where we were when she first named it. I was living in an apartment complex. We were walking through the parking lot.

"They told me I have Hodgkin's disease," she said.

I happened to know what that was. I could tell by the way she said it that she did not. It is one of the most curable forms, but cancer is cancer. I decided I should not be the one to tell her, or maybe it was that I didn't know how. She was 21.

It was a Friday. She did not find out until she went back home on Monday. It took me a while to get over that weekend. It's unsettling to be around someone with cancer when you know and they don't.

Now, several years later, she was telling me by phone she needed another biopsy.

"I don't know why I'm talking to you about it," she said. "I guess because I went through it with you the first time."

"It's just a biopsy," I said. "It's been eight years. You beat it."

"I know," said Christine. "It's just that everything's been going so good."

I asked about the symptoms. She said a shoulder had been sore for weeks. There was discoloration and swelling. It didn't fit with Hodgkin's; their theory was a reaction to the old radiation treatments she'd had.

What worried her, she said, is that the initial tests hadn't proved it benign, and oncologists were now involved.

"It looks like somebody beat me," she said. "I'm all black and blue. Maybe I'll check into the battered wife program at the Y."

Hearing it again reminded me of how much I'd missed that laugh.

The summer we were together, she had radiation for over a month. She did not lose much hair, but was tired much of the time. We tried not to talk about it. Instead, we joked of the way her relatives kept giving her these tragic stares.

"Adults," she would say, and roll her eyes. "They take things so seriously." We were young, and everything was possible and we figured if you ignored the pain, it would go away.

It worked most of the time, though once, late at night, suddenly, she started to cry.

"What's the matter?"

"Nothing. I'm sorry. I'm just being silly."

Then she said she was not being silly, she was afraid. We talked into the night. Finally, she said she felt better for having faced things, and ended the talk with a joke.

Now, over the phone, I reminded her of how we used to push it back with humor.

"I know," she said. "My mother used to say, 'I don't think you're dealing with it.' And I'd say, 'Dealing with what?' "

But she did deal with it, when she was ready, on her terms.

"It's different this time," she said. "I have my two kids; I have Nathan; I have my career."

"You sure you're not just covering up for the fact that you're in the Y right now."

"How'd you know?"

Toward the end of that earlier summer, I began to ask myself how I'd have reacted if it was me. Not well. It helped me see that what she had underneath was stronger than what I had.

I remember a moment from that time. The doctors had drawn heavy lines on her back to use as guides for the radiation machine. They told her she had to keep the markings until the treatments were over. One night, she told me the lines had begun to fade. She asked if I'd help. I took out a magic marker and slowly began tracing them over.

It was the one time it almost got to me. I knew if I showed it, it would have been unhelpful to her, but my hand went unsteady, and my throat thickened, and then she rescued me.

"Be careful," she said. "That tickles."

Over the phone, she told me she had to go. I told her that was typical and reminded her of the time she hung up on me after a fight.

"Oh, Patinkin," she said. "That was your fault."

"What did I do?"

"You never remembered my birthday."

"You're right." I said. "I'm sorry."

"Well thank you for saying that."

"When is your birthday anyway?"

"Patinkin."

At first, I was going to wait for the diagnosis before writing this. Then I decided that doesn't matter. It is not what this is about. It's about how to face hard things. Christine taught it well.

①

SHE'D BE PROUD OF THE WAY HE BECAME A MOTHER, TOO

I had not seen him since the funeral. He pulled into my driveway just after dusk. He'd been on call at the emergency room that morning, and the drive from Albany took him over four hours.

It was not the kind of weekend company I was used to. Normally, when friends come by late, it's not hard to run out for dinner. It's a bit different when you're single, as I was at the time, and hosting a young father with two babies.

We kind of half-embraced, which I'm usually not comfortable doing with men, but when you've been through something together, the shaking of hands seems almost cold.

"A station-wagon," I said. "Looks like you're coming down with middle age." He smiled and nodded at my car.

"You try squeezing two kids into a Rabbit."

Nate carried in the crib, I carried the walker, we both took an armload of diapers. His daughter had just turned one and his son two. He laid them on the couch, arched an eyebrow and asked if I wanted to help with the changing.

"I'd love to," I said. "But my bursitis."

"You're going to have to know about this stuff one day."

"Don't rush me." I volunteered for kitchen duty instead. When the children's mother was around, Nate and I had spent our share of afternoons in exercise rooms, competing at the bench-press. Now we were both playing mother ourselves. Things change.

It was an unlikely friendship. We had a woman in common. Her name was Christine. She and I were close for a year when I was younger. It ended between us when we moved to separate cities. There were a few months of silence, as there usually is when something ends, but we soon got back in touch, and I remember trying to start things up again when she told me about him.

"Well," she said. "The thing is, I'm getting married."

"Married?" I said. "Can't we at least have a weekend together first?"

"Oh, Patinkin," she said.

Soon, I got a letter announcing Matthew, and another for Kara, and then, last January, I got a phone call. She called from the hospital. I forget which word she used, but it was either incurable or terminal. She said that only 50 people come down with it a year. Then she said Nate could explain it to me better. She handed him the phone. It was the first time the two of us talked.

We finished dinner around 10, each of us holding a baby as we ate. He was much better at it than I. "Practice," he explained.

We put them to bed around 10 and went downstairs. For more than an hour, we talked of other things, mostly his doctoring. He'd just finished residency, and had decided on the emergency room as a specialty. Maybe a practice would come later, but for now, having normal hours was important—the kids, he said. I asked if they were showing it at all.

"No," said Nate. "They seem to be doing pretty good. They're young."

"Does Matthew ask for her ever?"

"He says mommy a lot. Mommy hoppital. He recognizes her picture."

It was one of the rarer forms of cancer. They gave her six weeks. She made it six months. She was 29.

The next morning, I walked into the kitchen to find scrambled eggs everywhere, including the curtains. The dog was licking them off Matthew's forehead. Kara was holding an open jar of parmesan cheese upside down. In the midst of this, Nate quietly read the paper. It was a lesson in fatherhood. When small children come into your life, order goes out, and the key is to not notice. I asked why Kara was chewing on a watermelon rind. He explained that it was the nearest thing, then went back to the paper.

I kept thinking this was not the way things were meant to fall. Women, I suppose, often handle this kind of burden, but there's something unlikely about a male left alone with babies. Maybe a male with children, but not babies.

We went to Newport, by the ocean, for the day. We must have looked strange walking down the crowded tourist streets: Two men, one with an infant on his back, the other with a stroller. We got our share of looks. Eventually, we headed for the water and found a place on some rocks. There's something about staring at surf that brings out talk.

"I think my biggest concern is for Kara," he said. "Matt'll be fine. He's outgoing, like she was. He had Chris around for a year and a half. He's a male, I'm a male. There's a role model. I don't know about Kara."

I threw a stick into the waves. The dog swam after it.

"I sure don't want to go mother shopping," said Nate. "Or even dating."

I asked if the nurses had begun circling. He laughed.

"I've had a few calls," he said.

"Already? Like what do they say?"

"Like, 'I'm here if you need me.' Or, 'I'm available.' "

"At least they're subtle," I said. "I wonder what Chris would say if she heard about this."

Nate smiled.

" 'See?' "

We got home late. We didn't get the kids upstairs until 11. When we left the room, they both, of course, began crying. We looked at each other, shrugged, and went back in, each sitting on a bed, waiting for them to drift off.

The room was almost dark. As we sat, I added up the time. It had been two months since the funeral.

"The kids at all difficult?" I said.

"Not really," he said. "Sometimes, you kind of miss adult company, you end up talking a lot of baby talk, but it helps having them."

No one said anything for a few seconds. He kept his stare on the crib.

"It ever get to you?" I asked.

"Sometimes."

"Nights?"

"More days. When they're both crying, and I can't do anything to make them okay, and there's no one else."

I asked the best way to handle those feelings. "Do you let it happen?" I said. "Or push it back?"

"You have to at least try pushing it back. Otherwise, it'd be the only thing you think about."

He said there is a hardest part. He keeps thinking about the last day. He wished he knew the hour it was coming. You always feel bad if you don't get a goodbye in.

The dog was licking scrambled eggs off Matthew's forehead again when I came into the kitchen the next morning. Kara was chewing on a pen.

"Why is she doing that?" I asked.

He explained that it was the nearest thing. We talked for a while about setting up a bench-pressing rematch soon. Then he looked at his watch and said it was time.

He carried out the crib, I carried the walker, there were far fewer diapers. I watched the car disappear down the block, thinking she'd be proud of him.

⏲

MY POLITICALLY CORRECT RESOLUTIONS

Belated New Year's resolutions, politically correct edition:

■ To stay fit, ideally through a universal health care system that gives equal medical attention to all, means notwithstanding.

■ To enjoy looking at simple seasonal pleasures, like the image of "womyn" in white summer dresses.

■ Though "glancing" would be more appropriate, as looking could be construed as objectification and exploitation.

■ To read more books, stressing those that underscore how each of society's disparate groups have a valid world view given their unique experiences.

■ Except, perhaps, straight white males.

■ To renew my commitment to marriage, an institution that should be open to all, genders of the parties notwithstanding, unless they choose not to enter so traditional an arrangement, prone as it is to dominance and servitude.

■ To watch less television, except for PBS.

■ To take my wife out more, not that she isn't equally capable of initiating outings, being an equivalent partner unbound by orthodoxy concerning which gender leads.

■ I meant the word "outings" in the traditional sense.

■ Not that tradition is the superior construct; very much the opposite.

■ To read more fairy tales to my children, except those with a patriarchal message implying females should expect rescue rather than relying for self-support on their own capabilities.

■ To watch more family movies; while keeping in mind there is no preferred definition of a legitimate family, nuclear being only one of many choices.

■ To make time for lazy weekend drives, preferably on public transit to avoid consumption of nonrenewable fossil fuels.

■ To join a Neighborhood Crime Watch group, but remembering that most criminals are victims themselves of a deprived upbringing foisted on the underprivileged by the dominant culture.

■ To help more chronologically challenged citizens of both genders cross the street.

■ As well as the differently abled.

■ Unless such a gesture were perceived as patronizing.

■ I resolve to get back to tennis and skiing, at the same time recognizing one shouldn't overly embrace sports that have been resistant to multi-ethnic participation.

■ To donate more to agencies helping the economically marginalized help themselves.

■ While remembering that they are marginalized through no fault of their own, being victims of a multi-generational dependent lifestyle.

■ Not to mention a downsizing corporate culture that exports jobs to low- wage countries at the expense of the American worker.

■ Then again, not putting jobs in the developing world betrays a chauvinistic myopia exacerbating the rich-poor global gap.

■ And by "developing" I don't mean that "developed" Western industrial states, with their emphasis on Darwinian capitalism, are superior.

■ To respect our country and flag, while keeping in mind that many peoples see us as expansionist oppressors, understandable given their own deprivations and aspirations.

■ I resolve to celebrate more family rituals while emphasizing to the pre-adults in my home that the holidays stressed by mainstream America are no more important than the less-known rites of other peoples.

■ Or species.

■ Finally, next year, to finish New Year's resolutions on Dec. 31, rather than days after as I'm doing now, not that chronic lateness is a character flaw, as it often results from adult attention deficit disorder, correctable with Serotonin-selective re-uptake inhibitors.

⊕

A Song of America

I was at a high school graduation. The principal asked everyone to stand for the anthem. I watched the students as they got to their feet. Unlike the parents, who stood straight, staring proudly, the kids were awkward. Some of the boys looked at each other and snickered. When you're 18, it's uncool to have to act so serious and patriotic.

It brought back memories.

I was equally uncomfortable when they played the anthem in high school, maybe more. It was hip to be down on America then. There was an unpopular war, an unpopular president, and a popular subculture based on healthy disrespect for authority. Getting emotional over the flag was the height of uncool.

I thought I'd always feel that way. Then, as a journalist, I began to travel to difficult places. Often, you have to leave America to understand America.

I went to Ethiopia one year to write about famine. I started to arrange a trip to one of the hunger camps. I was immediately told I could go nowhere without a government assigned "minder." His job was to make sure I only saw things the government wanted me to see. Before leaving, I had to go the Ministry of Censorship to have my film approved.

My next stop was the Sudan. I wrote a story about the drought and went to the hotel's front desk to send it back to America. The manager there, a state official, read what I'd written and said he wouldn't allow me to send it. Too critical of the government, he explained.

I'd always taken freedom of expression for granted. That trip taught me it is the exception, not the rule.

Two years later, I was in Northern Ireland to write about religious violence. In Belfast, I was shocked to find a city divided by huge walls called Sectarian Interfaces. They run a mile long and 30 feet high, made of concrete and steel. The walls are there to keep the two faiths apart. It's all Catholic on one side, all Protestant on the other.

One day, I met a Protestant minister who'd been expelled by his congregation in a small Northern Ireland city because he made an unacceptable gesture: He walked into a Catholic church to wish the people there a Merry Christmas. I asked the minister why that would offend anyone. He told me I wouldn't understand; Americans like me don't realize how unique our country is. There is perhaps no other nation on Earth, he told me, where different faiths coexist as peacefully as in my own.

In 1986, I went to Beirut, crossing the Green Line to the Moslem side. I was told that the all Americans there were prime targets for hostage taking. I asked if the government couldn't help me move around safely. Those I asked ended up laughing. There was no government to protect me; the city was run by extremist militias. If I was kidnapped, I was told, there was no police force that would be able to search for me. This wasn't America, they said. In Lebanon, there was no such thing as freedom from fear.

In 1989, Communism began to collapse in Eastern Europe. I made it to Berlin before the wall fell. One day, I stood by its thickest part, staring up while East German soldiers patrolled the top of it, unsmiling, rifles ready, showing me what an unfree world looks like.

In Czechoslovakia, I met a man who was a Ph.D. in physics but had been forced to work eight years as a furnace stoker. He told me that was typical. People who dared criticize the government were fired by the state from good jobs and given menial ones. He was lucky, really. Many like him were in prison.

One more memory: I traveled to Romania when Nicolae Ceausescu was still in power. They called him the Last Stalin. I took a cab to the home of a dissident. Secret police stopped me a block from his door, followed me to my hotel, then put me in the back of an unmarked car. At the airport, two security men questioned me for hours in a locked room before expelling me on the next plane out of the country. As I lifted off the Bucharest runway, I thought: "I cannot wait to get back to America." Lose freedom once, you treasure it forever after.

There in the high school gymnasium, while the anthem played, I thought back to those moments. Soon, the music ended. The students appeared relieved, their faces seeming to ask what was so special about the American flag. With these words, I wanted to tell them. ☯

REVENGE OF THE TELEMARKETEE

I'd been hoping to do this for years: At last, I turned the tables on a telemarketer.

Not that most are bad. Very tough way to make a living, cold-calling. Wouldn't have the fortitude to face it myself. But we all know the too-pushy kind. In my experience, one breed has been the pushiest: Out-of-town brokers. This was one.

"Hello, Mark, I'm sure you remember me." He gave a name I'd never heard before. Then he said his firm was the very one that gave—he paused for dramatic effect—Thomas Edison money for the lightbulb.

I wanted to say "Right decade, wrong century," but I didn't have time because he got right to it.

"I promised to touch base only when I had something exceptional in the market."

I opted for the two-kids-waiting-for-dinner-and-a-baby-in-my-arm defense.

"I wish I could talk, but I've got two kids waiting for dinner and a baby in my arm . . ."

"I understand, Mark, but I have a situation that's been developing more quickly than anticipated. Something you absolutely need to know about."

"Could you leave a number, I'll get back to you?"

"Now's the time, Mark. Focus on this. The name of the company is Republic Bank Corporation. Stock trades at 11 1/2 a share. Roughly two points off its yearly low."

"Great. But I'm trying to heat a bottle and cook Spaghetti-Os at the same time . . ."

"Stay with me, Mark, here are the nuts and bolts. Republic is the most profitable mid-sized bank in the country—$1.3 billion in assets. But the key is their earnings and revenue growth: 50 percent a year for the past three years."

Because my mother raised me to be polite on the phone, I was trapped. But then an idea hit me: Play Jimmy the Dunce.

"Fifty percent growth a year?" I said. "Is that good or bad?" From his end, brief silence. "Sir?," I said. "Hello?"

"Uh, here. Good or bad? Mark—it's unbelievable. Mark, I called to make money. This is how it's done. We believe the bank will be sold within eight weeks, probably half that. Based on an average multiple to book value, the company is worth $20 to $22 a share, but it's only trading at $11.50."

"Sounds like a bad deal then."

"What? Mark—it's the opposite. When this company is sold—soon—do you know what'll happen to its value? And your investment?"

"Why would anyone buy a company whose stock is so low?"

More silence. I could almost hear him thinking: "Is this guy really this stupid?" The dunce routine was working.

"Mark, we're talking 50 percent earnings growth . . ."

"I'd just be more comfortable buying in if the stock equaled the bank's worth. Or was higher."

"Mark, that's backwards. Focus. The whole goal is to buy low. That's where you get the upside. Look Mark, here's the clincher: Have you ever heard of Jerry Campbell?"

"Jerry Campbell? Don't tell me. Rings a bell."

"Mark, give me a chance to talk here. I'm getting to who he is."

"Wait—doesn't he play that nerdy detective on NYPD Blue? . . . Hello?"

". . . No. He doesn't."

"I swear: He's the one having the affair with Donna Abandando, the receptionist. Actually, the last episode, she broke it off . . ."

"Mark . . ."

No way I was going to let him break my rhythm. I was on a roll. "Tell you the truth, it's the one part of the show that isn't believable. Why would someone as gorgeous as Miss Abandando get involved with this wimpy detective played by Jerry Campbell?"

". . . Mark, that's not who Jerry Campbell is. Mark, when's the last time you bought a stock?"

"I have a good portfolio. General Motors. AT&T. Boeing."

"Great. So you're a blue-chip investor. Well, Republic is a blue-chip bet if you jump in now . . ."

"My grandmother bought a few shares of each for me when I was a kid. I still have them . . . Sir?"

"Here. Is that all you have invested in common stock?"

"Yes, but it's not like I have only one or two shares."

"That's good then."

"She got me 10 shares of each. My mother keeps the certificates for me in a safe deposit box."

"Really. What about mutual funds and bonds?"

"Frankly, I don't even know what a bond is."

"Well, Mark. Buy Republic, okay? Nice talking to . . ."

"Hey wait. I think I will buy. How about five shares?"

"To be honest, Mark, five shares isn't a level my company's capable of working with. And I've got another call . . ."

"Fine, I'll make it 10 shares."

"Mark, I don't want to hold you, didn't you say you had dinner going?"

"Forget dinner. I want to talk about this . . ."

"Mark, I've really got another call . . ."

"Put them on hold. How many years did you say this bank's had 50 percent growth?"

"Thanks for your time, Mark . . ."

"Wait—you've talked me into it. If it's good enough for Jerry Campbell of NYPD Blue, it's good enough . . ."

Click.

"Hello sir? Mr. Broker sir?"

Gee. Did I drive the poor guy so nuts he had to hang up?

Pity.

I DON'T GET THE 'POOR ME'S'

He'd just finished his sidework in the restaurant kitchen, putting salad plates in the cooler, washing the breadboards with bleach water, then readying his station for dinner by putting out silver. It's part of Gerry Collins' routine as waiter. He works at the Spaghetti Warehouse.

I met him a few months before when he waited on my table. I remember thinking that he seemed old for the job, over 50. I asked him how he liked the work. He said it was new for him; he'd spent his career as a computer engineer but had been laid off.

His story stayed on my mind. The other day, I decided to call, and yes, he was still there and would be happy to talk.

We sat together in the empty dining room. He's a thin man, polite, his gray hair well-groomed. He seemed tired. "Lunches are hard," said Gerry, "because you have to be quick. People are in a hurry."

A woman with a nametag that said Karleen paused briefly as she walked by and put her hand on his shoulder. "He's one of our best," she said.

"The kids here treat me well," he told me after she'd gone.

The kids?

Most of the workers are 18 to 25, he said. "I get my hugs from them every day. They treat me like a father."

He was laid off from his computer job four years ago. For a while, he sold televisions. "But I was on commission," said Gerry, "and didn't like making my living fighting with five other guys."

He kept sending out applications to computer companies, but did not make headway, so he decided to try being a waiter, temporarily. He did not expect to be at it this long. It's been a year.

Does he like it?

"I do, very much," he said. "I was employee of the month once. And I saved a guy's life about a year ago. He was choking."

He worked in computers 29 years, starting just after coming back from Vietnam in the mid-'60s. In time he rose to field engineer, with 28 people under him. He ran a kind of high-tech SWAT team, fixing big computer systems in companies.

"The president of Traveler's would call and say, 'I'm down. What are you going to do about it?' " Gerry recalled. Whatever the hour, he would fix it. He made more than $50,000 a year.

"When I got laid off," said Gerry, "I decided to take some time. I felt burned out. We'd been through a few hostile takeovers; part of the '80s. But I wasn't comfortable drawing benefits because I was able to work; I'm an accomplished cabinetmaker. So I went through my severance and retirement."

He and his wife have four children, two grown, and two 10 and 11. They had the younger ones because they didn't like an empty nest.

He worked for Computervision during the early 1980s, driving 60 miles from his home in Rhode Island to Bedford, Mass. on the outskirts of Boston. Then Prime Computer bought the company and reassigned him to Hartford, Conn., a two hour drive.

They put him up in a hotel during the week, tough lifestyle, but he loved the job. It was up to him to merge the two field engineering offices. "I had two beepers on my belt," he said. "I was on 24-hour call. I have a good work philosophy: I'm not afraid of it."

He was proud of how well he knew the machines. He began when the industry was still young. "Back when it was vacuum tubes and iron," said Gerry. For three decades, he worked on the technology as it evolved. "I got pretty darn good at what I did," he said. "I was working on $6 million systems and had $15,000 signature authority."

Doesn't that count for anything today?

"I'm still sending resumes out," he said. "But you end up talking to 24-year-old kids who don't know where I'm coming from."

Does he plan to keep applying?

"Oh yes. I'm not going to give up." He says he's sent out several thousand applications. "That's no exaggeration. But that's indicative of the times. You go to a job fair now, and there's no room for parking."

He feels he might have better prospects elsewhere—the Carolinas, or perhaps Texas; things are bad in New England, especially in high technology. But his in-laws are here, living just behind him. "They worked hard all their lives," says Gerry. "They have a right to see their grandkids."

The companies he's applied to have all been gracious, sending back nice letters. And though he feels his experience should mean more, he understands most managers have hundreds of applicants for each job, and that he's a man over 50 up against younger people with master's degrees.

I asked about the day he got laid off.

"I knew it was coming," said Gerry. "It wasn't only myself." He had to lay off some of his own people in the first wave. Downsizing, he said.

At first he wasn't worried. He presumed he could drive up to the high-tech belt around Boston and get a new job at will. But he found that almost every company was doing the same thing Prime was; firing, not hiring.

"I'd go to job fairs," said Gerry, "see friends in the same situation, and the lines would be so long, we'd break off, have a cup of coffee and try to come up with another strategy."

As we talked, Karleen came by again, asking if we wanted refills. "Yes, Karleen," he said. "Thank you for your kindness." She headed toward the kitchen. "She's one of our head-waits," he explained. "Very nice lady."

Soon more coffee was there. Gerry stressed that he's not bitter. "I'm more surprised," he said. "I didn't expect things would be so hard at this age."

He works from 9:30 to 3 as a waiter, then from 3:30 to 8 repairing electronic appliances for a retailer. Still, his income is a fraction of what he made in computers.

"But I do like it here," said Gerry. "I don't get the 'Poor Me's.' I've seen a lot of guys in my position get depressed. They go from $50,000 a year to $10,000 and it destroys their lives. But I like it here. I help the kids and they help me. Some of them come in with such a bright attitude it kind of rubs off. I don't have the 'Poor Me's.' "

Is there anything about being a waiter that's hard?

"Well," he said, "I've had diners ask me why don't I get a real job. My answer is I'm not selling drugs. This is honest work. I pay my taxes, though it might not be as big a cut."

Soon it was time for him to go. We went through the kitchen, where he showed me his work. He pointed out the salad bar, which he'd set up, and the 75 breadboards he'd just cleaned. There was a big sign on the wall with three questions: "Is it hot? Does it look good? Are you proud to serve it?" Gerry said he always made sure he could answer yes to all three.

Then it was time to go. At the door, he saw that it was raining hard. He buttoned his coat all the way up. Then, a man of his times, he headed off to his second job.

🕐

I AM WHAT I'M NOT

I just saw a glimpse of the way people such as me—white people—are likely to be referred to in the America of the near future, and it's unsettling. I was thumbing through the Brown University Alumni Magazine and came across a chart of the new freshman class. It was broken down by ethnic group.

There were African-Americans, Asian Americans, Hispanics, Native Americans, and finally, there was the category I'd fall under.

White? No. White apparently is now passé. Caucasian? Not even that. I've become something else. Something new.

I'm a . . . drum roll please . . . non-minority.

I've never heard that one before. But there it is. My new label.

Obviously, the world's point of view has changed. Americans used to be classified either as whites or non-whites, which I'd be the first to acknowledge was a bit insulting. Non-whites? Sounds almost colonialist. I can't imagine it's a good message for African-American kids to grow up hearing themselves defined as "non-whites," as if they're "non" what they should be. I'm glad we've moved beyond that.

But now it has gone the other way. Suddenly, after a lifetime of being cast as the benchmark class, it's me who is "non" what I should be. A non-minority.

I suppose this comes under the heading of political correctness. We're in an age when white people—particularly white males—are being reassessed. We're no longer seen as the group who built the country; the new view is that we dominated it. Frankly, there's some truth to that. Therefore, white folks aren't exactly seen as trendy these days. The phrase "white people" itself is no longer a label of pride.

Ask any black person and they'll tell you they're proud to declare themselves an African-American. Same goes for Asian Americans, Latinos and Native Americans. But ask someone like me what we consider our central identity, and we won't exactly stand up proudly and declare, "I'm a white person."

Still, we are what we are, nothing we can do about it, and I figured that even if the phrase "white person," "white American" or "whites" will never be politically correct, at least it'll remain our official label. What else could we possibly be called?

But suddenly, on this particular survey in this particular magazine, they couldn't even bring themselves to print the word. The implication is that the word "white" is no longer acceptable to say.

I can picture the editor frowning over it, then making a decision: "We'll have to change this. I don't want a word evoking oppressors in my magazine."

"Then what'll we call them? Caucasians?"

"Almost the same thing. We can do better."

"I've got it. Non-minorities."

I guess it's only just. As I said, after decades of minorities being defined by what they weren't—non-whites—it's now our turn. The problem is that I'm sure it won't stop here. In addition to being a politically incorrect race, I'm a politically incorrect gender, too.

So, soon I'll doubtless see an article or survey referring to my sex not as "men" but . . . drum roll again . . . non-females. Or more likely, non-women.

The more I think about it, the more I realize I fit into other politically incorrect categories, such categories being defined as any non-oppressed class.

In future surveys, if downsizing doesn't get me, I'll also be non-jobless. And a non-single-parent. Who had a non-unhappy childhood.

It's a disturbing thought to put all these things together, but let me try: I'm a non-minority, non-woman who is non-lower-income, a non-single-parent and the product of a non-unhappy-childhood.

It's downright embarrassing is what it is.

I promise to try to do better

☺.

IT IS NICE, HE SAID, TO BE REMEMBERED

They are trying hard to keep this gathering a tradition, even though it is getting difficult, with most of them older now. The women brought pastries, and one a big chocolate cake, and if you listened to the conversations, most were about the same thing. They spoke of grandchildren, partly because it is that time of life, but there was another reason, which had to do with what brought them here.

This being a holiday celebration, it is their tradition to light candles, but someone forgot them, so they had to rummage around until they found some old ones that were half burned down and they settled for those.

David Newman, who is 70ish, watched as the match touched each wick. "We're getting smaller," he said. "Pretty soon there won't be anyone left to tell the story."

I asked him what camp he had been in. He rolled up his sleeve and showed me a tattooed number: 16558. "Auschwitz," he said. Then he said he wanted to introduce me to someone, his grandson Michael. "This is what we live for," he told me. The grandchildren, he said, are a symbol that the Nazis did not succeed. I glanced at the chocolate cake on the table. "Happy Hanukkah," it said. "Rhode Island Holocaust Survivors."

I asked why he has not had the tattoo removed. "Some people say there was no Auschwitz," Newman said. "That is why."

He told me a story of coming home from a friendly poker game on a recent summer night, and being pulled over for speeding. He knew he was guilty and waited for the ticket but then the policeman caught sight of the number on Newman's arm. He asked if Newman had been in a concentration camp. Newman said he had. The policeman closed his ticket book. "Mr. Newman," he said, "Please slow down. You lived through that. Please don't speed." Newman wishes now he had gotten the policeman's name so he could thank him, not for the break; for remembering. So few, he said, seem to remember.

There were perhaps 35 people here. A few stood to make welcoming remarks. In the background, the youngest children talked, some rather loudly. No one minded.

I approached a man who introduced himself as Henry Szynkarsky. Had he been in a camp? He shook his head. He was lucky, he said; a Polish farmer let him hide for four years in his basement. He wanted the farmer's name known: Stefan Kesik. He was a Catholic. Had this Catholic been found hiding Jews, said Szynkarsky, the Nazis would have killed his family and burned his house. Others, listening, nodded. Their a story, one said, is of a dark time but also, in a few cases, of the human spirit at its noblest.

I sat at a table to do more interviews, but at first was unable to. A woman with a number tattooed on her arm brought me some potato pancakes, which I tried to decline, but she insisted on wrapping them for me to go. Another did the same with some pastries.

The talk around me was mostly of today, but when I began to probe, they started sharing stories. Two women found they'd been among the last on the death camp trains out of Czechoslovakia. They shared stories about four days in closed cattle cars, hundreds packed so tightly the dead remained standing. Others spoke of being pulled away as they tried to hold to their mothers' dresses at the selection. Then they spoke of the Americans, the soldier boys, their rescuers; they will never forget them.

At last it was time to go. Heinz Samdelowski thanked the organizers, and then he did something that slightly embarrassed me. He looked my way and said he wanted to thank me most of all. It meant so much that someone from the media cared enough to come, he said. Sometimes, he explained, it seems no one on the outside remembers. It is nice, he said, to be remembered.

🕐

TV HABITS

The Nielsen company has decided it needs to better monitor the habits of TV viewers, so it's planning to test a new system that— true story—will let it watch us through our own TV sets. Supposedly, it will allow Nielsen not only to tell what shows viewers have turned to, but when they leave the room and even when they glance at a newspaper.

To get an idea of what this will mean, I decided to record my own TV watching habits for a night. If I'm at all typical, Nielsen is in trouble. They're going to have to rate shows not by the half hour, but the minute. Or less. The combination of 60 channels and a remote control has reduced my attention span to almost nothing.

My report:

8 p.m.: Pick up Cable Guide, study all 60 channels and decide there's nothing on. Turn on television anyway and start to flip randomly. Finally stop on Channel 40 to see Elvis in "Love Me Tender." Get bored after five minutes and head into kitchen for Hostess Ding Dong.

8:15 p.m.: As TV drones in background, I place Ding-Dong on coffee table, then realize I forgot glass of ice water. Go back into kitchen for it, then return to find dog eating Ding-Dong. Yell at dog, then go back for second Ding-Dong.

8:20 p.m.: Turn on headline news. Sports is on, which doesn't hold my interest, so I pick up Time magazine, opening it to people section where I read about Di. TV drones in background.

8:25 p.m.: Look back at TV and begin flipping channels. Pause on show, or possibly infomercial, called "Can You Beat Baldness?" Decide I can't and continue flipping.

8:28 p.m.: Wife asks if it's absolutely necessary to flip from channel to channel. Can we please pick one and stop?

8:29 p.m.: I stop immediately, finding I've landed on The Three Stooges. I drive wife to further distraction by doing my impersonation of Curly: "Oh, a wise guy?" Then commercial break comes on.

8:30 p.m.: Another glance at guide convinces me there's still nothing on. Head into kitchen to get Cheez Balls.

8:36 p.m.: Cannot enjoy Cheez Balls without flipping so I begin doing so—from food channel to weather channel to C-SPAN. Wife says my flipping is giving her a headache.

8:42 p.m.: Stop on MTV. A group called "Fine Young Cannibals" is playing. Declare to wife that there's been no decent music since 1972.

8:43 p.m.: Turn back to headline news, then pick up Newsweek magazine, turning to people section, where I read about Prince Charles. TV drones in background.

9 p.m.: Return from kitchen with bowl of microwave popcorn. Refer again to TV guide. Still nothing. Pick up remote anyway and start flipping.

9:05 p.m.: Pause on nature show. Narrator says I'm watching the mating dance of the western grebe. Resume flipping.

9:15 p.m.: I briefly watch the Mandrell sisters hosting country music awards, turn to Murphy Brown and try MTV one more time. It's Bon Jovi. Wife asks if it's absolutely necessary to watch Bon Jovi. Flip back to headline news, which is now getting very familiar, and pick up people section of U.S. News and World Report, where I read about Fergie. TV drones in background.

9:30 p.m.: Head to kitchen to retrieve Hostess Ring Ding. More flipping brings me to Donna Reed, which involves lovelorn Jeff falling for Mary's friend. Pause and pick up People magazine, where I read an overview of all the royals.

9:40 p.m.: Grow bored and start flipping again. Wife tells me she will need therapy if I don't settle on one channel and leave it there. I freeze on the Home Shopping Network, grow bored, then walk across room to get people section of morning paper. Return to find dog eating Ring Ding.

9:55 p.m.: Debate whether to go to bed. Pick up guide. Notice Telly Savalas will be narrating a tour of the Grand Canyon at 10, which should hold me until 10:05 at least. Meanwhile, for the fourth time, I turn to headline news. Then I discover tidbit in newspaper people section about Camilla Parker Bowles and start to read. TV drones in background. ☺

He asked why we hadn't written a story about the bikers.

What did they do? I asked.

"The toys thing," he said. "I'm a biker myself, and like I say, when we do wrong, nobody forgets; when we do right, nobody remembers."

What toy thing?

"We have a thing every year where two thousand of us ride with toys for kids that aren't making ends meet too much."

When was it?

"On Sunday. The way I see it, if there was a fight, it would have made the papers. But there wasn't, so nobody made a thing of it at all. Like the unsung heroes."

How many toys did you bring?

"We filled two 40-foot tractor-trailers. Everyone drove up with the toys strapped on their sissy bars."

What are sissy bars?

"You put them on the back so your old lady don't fall off."

What kind of toys did everyone bring?

"A lot of stuffed animals. I saw Wiley Coyote. I think Kermit the frog was on one of them. There was so much; it was like—phew."

You're one of the bikers?

"Yeah."

What do you drive now?

"Nothing right now. I had an accident. I broke my knee."

How?

"I don't want to get into that. Can't you make this a nice story? About the unsung heroes. Every bike club isn't an outlaw organization, like people think. They do good."

What kind of motorcycles were there?

"A lot of Harley Davidsons. They're American-made. Built for Americans, by Americans."

That's why you buy them?

"Yeah, we like to keep it in our own country."

What kind of Harleys?

"Low-Riders, Super-Glides, Soft-Tails, Sportsters, Wide-Glides, Panheads and a couple of Flatheads."

They sound like nasty bikes to me.

"They are—thunderbikes. But don't put that in."

I'd like to.

"Yeah, if you want, sure."

Was everyone dressed in leather?

"Yeah, but that doesn't make us radicals. We have jobs. We're not a bunch of bums."

A lot of beards?

"Hey—you gonna ride a motorcycle in November, you gotta have something on your face."

Why would two thousand bikers all bother?"

"Because we know about Christmastime in the lean times—when you're a kid and there's nothing under the tree."

I didn't think bikers had soft hearts.

"Aww, you'd be surprised."

I didn't think they liked children, either.

"Yeah, they do. They like dogs and puppies too, you know?"

Were you there on Sunday?

"I was in a truck with my buddy—a Ford 4-by-4. And my girl, and his girl."

What toys did you bring?

"Let's see, three dolls."

What kind?

"I don't know, dolls—baby dolls. And Pound Puppies."

What are Pound Puppies?

"Those are them wrinkly stupid-looking dogs, but my niece likes 'em, so I figured I'd get some for some other kids, too. Also some LEGO building block kits, and another stuffed dog that had a, like, winter-hooded jacket or something on it."

Could I ask your name?

"I don't know; I feel funny about it, I've never done this before. It's just that everybody said we didn't get any coverage or anything, so I thought I'd give it a shot."

How about a first name?

"I'll give you my nickname. Everyone knows it. Rufus."

How old are you, Rufus?

"Twenty-six."

How much money did you spend on toys?

"Probably about $50."

Why so much?

"It's hard to get into that."

I'd like to know.

"It's like, I don't have much of a family anymore, you know? So you feel, around Christmastime, if you don't got anyone, rather than put yourself in a negative atmosphere, you put it in a positive way. Does that sound all right?"

I told him it did. I told him I never thought bikers would end up reminding me what the season is all about.

☽

AND YOU THOUGHT "WAR AND PEACE" WAS A LONG BOOK

A **woman from Time-Life called.** She asked if I had a moment.

I'm against a lot of things, like cologne on men and cheek rouge on women, but I'm not against Time-Life doing a profile on me.

"Well," I said modestly, "I don't know why your readers would be interested. I'm just a local columnist. But sure, go ahead."

"That's very good, sir," the woman said. "We're calling because we thought you'd want to sample our Vietnam book series."

Once I got past the slight, I began to feel sorry for the woman. Anyone who makes a living interrupting other people's dinner must get a lot of rejection. Out of sympathy, I took the series. I figured it was only a few books.

That was a year ago. I'm now worried about my attic caving in. So far, 15 Vietnam books have come in, and there's no end in sight.

Time-Life has a way of doing this to people. They book you to death. It's easy to tell who's been victimized. They're the ones whose home libraries cover only three subjects. There are the 412 volumes on World War II, the 270 on Great Inventors 1900-1905, and the 185 volumes on how to cook fish.

There's one other tipoff. If you look closely, you can tell the books haven't been opened. The truth is, no one on record has ever read an entire Time-Life series. You'd have to quit your job and read full-time to do it.

Not that Vietnam isn't worth in-depth treatment. I could see three volumes. Five volumes, even. But 15—that's only so far—is getting up here. As was once pointed out, the story of creation was told in three inches of type.

My theory is that they have a quota. Some MBA in Time-Life's marketing department figured that 15 books would generate more income than three. He was right. I know. At $18 each, I'm closing on $300. And counting.

Anyway, once they finish this series, the MBA will doubtless send wor down to editorial to stretch it out some more. If there's anything American know how to do, it's stretch it out. School taught us that.

Remember how with term papers you kept coming up with bogus digressions to turn a one-page idea into the required 15-page length? As in "To examine the juxtaposition of violence and eroticism in Delacroix's art, we must first go back to his childhood. After that, we will discuss his early years. Then we will explore his youth. After that, we'll probe his teens..."

It's the same at Time-Life. If you look close, there are clear signs of stretching it out. One book in the Vietnam series is called "Thunder from Above." It's about bombs. Another book is called "Rain of Fire." It seems to be also about bombs. That's 400 pages on bombs. You have to really be into bombs.

I called Time-Life to see if any more were coming. I got their book spokeswoman, Joyce White. She told me no, Vietnam goes 15 books.

"Thank goodness," I said. "It's over, then."

"Wait a minute," she said. "I'm looking at the catalog. They added three more."

I asked her to double-check that. It's true. Midseries, they added three books. And never told us. I guess it's smart business, though consumers could be in trouble if other industries pick it up. I can see trying to buy a car under these conditions.

"We'll be adding a Taurus wagon to your Explorer sir."

"But I don't need a Taurus wagon. And it's an extra $18,000."

"I'm sorry, sir. The company's decided to add it."

I asked Joyce about other series. My favorite is "Home Repair"—36 volumes. I'll leave others to explore why fixing faucets merited twice the depth of our longest war.

Incidentally, I have the "Home Repair" series, bought it a few years ag when a Time-Life telemarketer I felt sorry for called during dinner and told me it would help me with odd jobs. Eventually, I started getting books on such subjects as how to replace a toilet. I debated sending that one back on the grounds there are some things I wouldn't do even if I was an expert, but the one thing Time-Life never tells you is how to return books, which is why we don't. Easier to just stack the things in the attic. Smart, those Time-Life people.

The other thing the "Home Repair" series never told me was how to build a book shelf, which was the one thing I eventually needed to make.

If I had to guess at their motto, it would be this: "Too much of a good thing, or even a mediocre thing, is profitable." That's why they cranked out 30 volumes on "The Old West," then 30 more—honest—under the heading "Classics of the Old West," and no doubt these will soon be followed by six more 30 volume sets to be called Keepsakes- Remembrances- Reminders- Mementos- Traces- and Vestiges-...Of The Old West.

To compare, Will Durant's epic series, "The Story of Civilization," is a third as many volumes as just the first Old West effort, though it covered a bit more ground than Dodge City. Edward Gibbon, who did about 12 volumes on the "Decline and Fall of the Roman Empire," would have been fired by Time-Life for writing too tight.

This all would have been a lot easier if that Time-Life caller of a year ago had simply wanted to do a profile on me.

Then again, knowing their style, they'd probably have ended up stretching my life's one paragraph worth of material into 22 volumes. At that length, despite it being her favorite subject, Time-Life's likeliest buyer for it—my mother—would just stack it in the attic.

🕐

A DEATH ON AMERICA STREET

I saw in the newspaper that Jackie Iavarone died at home on America Street this week. He left behind the family that raised him, but no family of his own; he never married.

The obituary was short. The only thing noted about Jackie's life was that he served in Vietnam in the Marine Corps. I almost turned the page but two things made me want to know more. First, there was a small photograph of Jackie as a clean-cut young man, white Marine dress hat, his face all hope and pride.

Then there was the address, America Street.

I called the home of Jackie's father. A friend answered and explained the father is elderly now.

And what about Jackie?

The friend paused. "We'd very rarely seen much of him," he said. "You know how grown boys are. He lived on his own. From here to there to there."

Then I called the state medical examiner. The cause of death: "Phenobarbitol, benzodiazepan and cocaine intoxication." There had been history of drug problems.

I drove to America Street. You hear a name like that and expect a tree boulevard, big houses, kids riding bikes. But it is mostly crowded tenements. I knocked at the address where I was told Jackie had a room; there was no answer.

The obituary said Jackie had one sister. I reached her at her home in a small town in Massachusetts.

"Yes," she said. "He was my younger brother." She had a calm, thoughtful voice and said she would be happy to talk.

She paused to retrieve his Marine training graduation book from Parris Island. He was in Platoon 393. He went to Vietnam in 1965 as a communications soldier. She thinks his Jeep hit a land mine.

"His arm was almost completely blown off," she said. They had to reattach it. He had skull, brain, face and leg injuries. He was in hospitals over a year, but he never really recovered.

"Afterward," said Joan, "there was no way he could ever work. He couldn't think clearly. He was on very heavy doses of anti-convulsive medications. He lived most of his life in pain. He really died in the Vietnam War."

I asked about Jackie as a boy. I could almost hear Joan smile over the phone.

"He was the straightest student in a Catholic high school," she said. "I thought he should go on to college, but he decided to fight for America. He thought he should help his country."

When they were younger, Joan worked at a neighborhood pharmacy, and she remembers Jackie coming in often and asking for a bowl of whipped cream, his favorite dessert. She also remembers that he was a Cub Scout.

After the war, he distanced himself.

"I'd say, 'Can I visit?' " Joan recalls. "He'd say, 'It would be better if we didn't.' " She did manage to see him from time to time; she recalls him shrunken in height from back injuries, limping from knee injuries, his face swollen from anti-convulsive drugs. He was in and out of veterans' medical programs.

"I think ultimately he became one of the homeless," says Joan. "With no reason. The background he comes from and the family he had—there was no reason. But he was ashamed of what had become of him. He didn't want to be remembered that way."

She asked that I put in the paper a plea: That others out there like Jackie should reach out for help. No one, she says, should have to live that way.

And a final thought: "He was never bitter," Joan said. "He always loved his country. And God."

Jackie Iavarone left us last week. He was a Cub Scout, a Marine and a homeless person. He died alone on America Street. He was 47. 🕐

TWISTED PHONE CORDS, POODLES IN SWEATERS AND SPOONS IN GARBAGE DISPOSALS

I was reading a New York Times obituary about a famous editor named William Shawn when I came across an unlikely sentence. It went this way: "He disliked crowds, fast driving, air conditioning and self-service elevators."

Until then, I'd never thought of dislikes as key to a person's legacy. But it makes sense, so when I go, I'd like whoever gets burdened with my obituary to consider a few things.

During his rather tedious, mostly uneventful life, Mr. Patinkin was known to dislike the following:

- Slow sink drains.

- Windshield ice.

- Trying to refold road maps.

- Not realizing you dropped a spoon down the garbage disposal until you've turned it on.

- The shampoo coming open in your travel kit.

- People who go 15 in a 45.

- Becoming aware of a ticking clock when you're trying to fall asleep.

- Restaurant tables with uneven legs.

- Running out of hot water in the shower.

- Twisted phone cords.

- Grocery bags that break just as you walk up the porch steps.

- Sweetbreads, named to fool diners into ordering thymus glands.

- Packing for trips where the weather is predicted to be between 40 and 80.

- CDs that skip.

■ Those thin plastic fasteners that hold tags on clothing.

■ Not to mention pins.

■ Being in a long supermarket aisle with no People magazine nearby.

■ When the bottom part of your tie comes out longer than the top.

■ Pistachio shells that have no openings.

■ The words "needs assembly."

■ Also, "Continued next week."

■ Bedsheets tucked in so far they don't reach higher than your chest.

■ My driver's license photo.

■ Childproof medicine bottles that are also adultproof.

■ Computers advertised for $1,000, a month after you bought the same model for $2,000.

■ Those padded envelopes filled with gray fluff.

■ Cards that fall out of magazines.

■ Poodles in sweaters.

■ Trying to free the sun-visor from its notch.

■ No pennies in your pocket when you need them; too many when you don't.

■ Getting the coat zipper stuck in that thin piece of fabric next to it.

■ Wrong-number callers who hang up in a huff, as though it's your fault.

■ Nothing good in the mail.

■ Sticky floors in movie theaters.

■ Bending the flip-top on a can without it opening.

■ Ice cream cones that start dripping from the bottom when you don't have a napkin.

■ The way they make the volume on commercials louder than the show.

- The words, "File not found."

- That high whining sound a mosquito makes when in your ear...

- ...slapping your own face hard to kill it...

- ...then hearing the same whining sound a minute later...and a minute after the next slap...and the next...and I have to stop this column because it's happening right now.

🕐

ROOTS

I just spoke with a friend I'd been out of touch with for a year, and he told me something not uncommon of my generation, or any American generation really: He'd moved again.

That makes 7 or 8 times in 20 years. The usual amount. I once saw a study saying most of us move nine times in a life. We move chasing the usual things: mates and jobs and comfort and opportunity. It's part of the national character. We celebrate the Huck Finns who yearn always to light out for the territory.

But there's an opposite American sentiment, just as true, that we don't celebrate often enough, which is why I still remember a man named Shorty Hutson I read about a few years back.

Shorty is a farmer in Illinois. He made the news one season when his corner of the world turned into flood country. His was the only homestead in his area that fended off the waters. Newspapers ran an aerial shot of his 2-acre farm compound: Green and dry surrounded by muddy waters.

He was spared not by luck, but work. He'd spent the last 20 years building his own levee, 6 feet high. He figured the Mississippi would crest sooner or later, and he didn't want it to wash away his roots. Before the flood of '92, his neighbors needled him about it. Not since.

This column is not, however, about a man who beat a flood. It's about something else in the tale of Shorty Hutson that got me thinking.

His dry, 2-acre compound includes a barn, a grain bin, a shed, two garages and Hutson's white house. It turns out that Shorty Hutson was born in that house over 70 years ago. His children were born there, too. They're grown now, and Shorty remains there with his wife. He never moved. Never wanted to.

"This is the old homestead," Shorty explained to a reporter. "You carry on where your father left off." His own father had done the same. Shorty's 125-acre farm was bought by his grandfather a century before.

So here we are, a generation that moves 5 to 10 times in 20 years and Shorty Hutson hasn't moved in three-quarters of a century. I should be dismissing him as a relic who has no adventure in him, but it's the opposite I think he understands something many of us don't.

A friend of his quoted in the newspaper story is named Loren Sinele. "He's a diehard," Sinele said. "Kind of like a lot of us out here on the prairie. The Good Lord put you there, there's where you're going to be."

If ever there was a philosophy about roots, that's one. In our mobile society, we don't exalt roots often, but along with his levee, roots are certainly what kept Shorty Hutson's life from being washed away.

It's not for everyone, can't be anymore, but I'll bet that by staying put, Shorty Hutson has found a kind of happiness many of us never know even though we chase it across America and back.

"The Good Lord put you there, there's where you're going to be."

Mark Twain, who authored Huck Finn and did as good a job as anyon capturing the American character, didn't write that line.

But you know, I'll bet he'd have been kind of proud if he had.

🕐

WHAT WOULD I DO WITHOUT COMPUTERS? A LOT.

How Computers Have Streamlined My Life:

8 a.m.—Boot up. I love my machine: 486 microprocessor, 12 MB ram, I'm armed. If Shakespeare had a Compaq Prolinea, he'd have written twice as many plays.

8:00:20—In Windows. For years I've been trying to get efficient; Windows is going to do it. Instead of a dozen projects lost in neglected files and piles, I've got everything on one screen. Today, I'll do a newspaper column, finish a book proposal, script an idea for a TV commentary and write a freelance piece. A lot to juggle, but with Windows, I can blaze between each with the click of the Alt-Tab combination.

8:10—You can't be efficient unless you're organized, and I've got the tool: A computer calendar. PIMs, they're called—Personal Information Managers. Think I'll peruse my To-Do List first. It's got about 30 items and I vow to myself to accomplish at least 25. Hmm, top-item: "Organize organizer." I begin to adjust my PIM's To-Do list, Goals List and Calls list, but abandon that when I discover I can load anniversaries, like family birthdays. I also see I can adjust my cardfile template and though I don't really need to—don't even know what a template is—I learn to adjust it anyway because...because I can. By the time I look up, it's 90 minutes later, and time well spent. I now know what a cardfile template is.

9:45—You don't want to do a column until you've got a fix on the news, but no problem; a few keystrokes, and I'm online. Great, I've even got e-mail waiting. From my brother in Chicago. He's writing to tell me his PIM is better than mine. No way. I spend 15 minutes writing back why he's wrong, then wait for a response. No response. Guess he's not online, so I call and tell him he's got e-mail waiting. He hangs up and soon, e-mails me back. We do this for over an hour. I love computers.

11:00—Before perusing the online news, I decide to ramp up my modem connection from 14,400 to 28,800 to speed browsing. I try, get error messages, switch to the online tech-help area, get instructions, tinker some more, but finally find there's no high-speed line from my city yet. I'll try tomorrow. Meanwhile, I stop by an online chat room where two dozen people can simultaneously type notes back and forth. For kicks, I try Teen Nook, where the messages are as follows: "Any California boys here?" "How about a Bud break?" And: "Bye, goin' surfin." Intrigued, I hang in for a while.

11:55—Being mature, I decide to find a chat room my own age. Here is—the Thirty-Something room. Almost, anyway. I find another called Over 40, and sign on. Suddenly, a box appears on my screen titled "Instant Message" from a person named Valerie who teaches me computer signs fc smiling and frowning, to be read sideways as follows. :) and :(...Cool.

1:05 p.m.—I at last go to the news areas of my online service and catc up on the latest. Then, on the main menu screen, I see it. The sign for the Internet. Can't resist. I spend an hour trying to navigate it, at last finding the access code for the White House Screen. Wow. I'm in the White House, at least virtually. It takes long minutes to download the screen. After staring endlessly at the hourglass icon that signifies a download's in progress, I get a picture of Bill and Hillary waving. Very cool. But I've got a column to write.

2:15—As I Alt-Tab toward my word-processor, I decide to peruse Quicken, the money planning package my wife has been using. I learn we are spending more than we're making. This inspires the Provider side of me, and I click to my freelance project so I can make side money. I tinker with an idea for 20 minutes, then realize the deadline for my column—my day job—is at hand.

3:00 —I write frantically under the gun, with only five side trips to the online service, including a pause to order Nickelodeon magazine for my daughter and a final nosy glance into the Teen Chat room.

5:30—Column finally done. I'm exhausted. Time to call it a day. But first I go back to my PIM to cross off all the To-Do projects I've completed. Not the 25 I'd hoped for, I'm afraid. In fact, only one, the column. I move everything else forward a day, and as I turn off the machine, a thought occurs to me.

I realize now why Shakespeare was so prolific. He didn't have a computer to distract him.

THE COLUMN I COULDN'T WRITE

There are many columns I set out to write but decide to shelve because the story doesn't turn out the way I expect.

An example:

It was going to be a great column. I'd come across an intriguing classified ad. It was placed by an elderly woman who said she'd been beaten up, and wanted to thank all those friends who'd helped her survive and hold onto her home.

It struck me as a great tale of neighborliness. A courageous older woman had been viciously assaulted by some criminal, and her community had stood by her. I pictured uplifting details, like medical bills her neighbors had helped pay so she wouldn't lose the house. I called and she invited me by.

It turned out to be a nice house in the suburbs. A short woman about 65 opened the door and waved me in. She made me tea and led me to a sitting room. I took out my notebook.

"Tell me about the assault," I said.

"Oh," she said, shaking her head. "They pushed me down. They hit me."

I asked how it happened. Walking at night? In the city? The parking lot of a mall? Some punks preying on her because she was old and an easy target?

It was a couple who claimed this house was theirs, she said, but it wasn't, it was hers.

"Pardon?" I said.

She spoke in a sweet, sincere voice. "They don't want me to stay here." Then she went into some elaborate explanation I couldn't follow about various complex claims on the house.

And they pushed you down?

Well, she said, they pushed her, anyway.

Suddenly, out of nowhere, another elderly woman walked right up to us. She had black circles under her eyes and a mean scowl. She did not say hello or introduce herself. She just said a single sneering sentence.

"My sister's a liar," she said.

"Your sister?" I said.

She pointed at the sweet elderly woman I was talking to.

"Her," the scowling woman said. "My sister. She's a liar."

Now the sweet one leaned close and whispered.

"She's not all there," she said to me. Then she took me into a big living room. There the plot thickened. There was an elderly man on a hospital bed with a nurse sitting nearby. The nurse nodded at me. The older lady and I sat on chairs as she continued her story.

"They did. They pushed me several times. They don't want me to live here."

Before I could ask a question, the scowling woman appeared again. She looked like a vision from a Stephen King movie.

"She's a liar," the woman said. Then she looked right at her sister. "You're a liar and you know it."

Suddenly, the elderly man in the hospital bed began to hack and gurgle. The nurse walked over to him and grabbed some tissue.

"Cough it up for me," she said.

The sweet woman took me by the hand and led me to another pair of chairs, but the scowling sister followed.

"Liar, liar, liar," she shouted.

I looked to the nurse for rescue. She gave a glance that said she wasn't about to get involved, and then the man in the bed started hacking again.

"Cough it up for me," said the nurse. "Let's go. You can do it."

"Liar," said the sister.

"Let's go sit in another room," said the sweet woman. But I told her I really had to be going. She gently took me by the wrist and said she wasn't done yet. This went on for a half-hour.

At last I managed to move toward the door. "My sister's a big fat liar," the scowling woman said.

"Thank you," I said, backing down the steps, across the lawn, toward my car. I opened the door. "Thank you both," I called. "It's really been great."

"She's a liar."

"Cough it up for me," said the nurse.

"Thank you all so much," I said.

I think the last time I popped a car's clutch and squealed away was in college. I hadn't lost my touch.

A NATION'S SOUL

I **went to Paris on vacation** and had the bad timing to be there on Bastille Day, France's July 4th. Only one thing happens in Paris on Bastille Day, a parade. Well, I thought, why not. I made it to the Champs Elysees early and waited for the floats and marching bands.

There were neither.

This is what I saw instead:

First came Army jeeps, followed by armored troop carriers, then half-tracks with mounted machine guns. The crowd applauded. The biggest applause was for the biggest guns. At one point, huge mobile radar units went by and then enormous tanks, hundreds of them, bringing the loudest cheers so far. This, I thought, had to be the climax.

It wasn't. The climax was missiles. The missiles were as big as trees. The asphalt shook.

My first reaction was that this wasn't the smartest tactical move. They must have put every weapon in France in this parade. If I were Ghadafi, I'd invade on Bastille Day.

My second reaction was more personal. Around me, a half-million Parisians cheered wildly, and it should have been infectious but all I felt was discomfort. It wasn't out of pacifism, that's not me anymore, it was something else. Unfamiliarity? Perhaps. I've seen a lot of parades in America but never one with tanks.

Which got me thinking. Why not? I suppose when you've got it, you don't have to flaunt it. Having never been conquered, we don't feel a need to rattle sabers. Still, we have pride in our might. Why not show it off?

Standing there on the Champs Elysees, I began to understand.

Because even though America has unequaled strength, that's not our soul. What makes American parades wonderful is that we don't celebrate how we defend ourselves, but what we're defending.

Look close at the best of our parades; That's America walking by. It's baton twirlers and high school marching bands; volunteer clubs, women's clubs and Rotary Clubs; it's clowns, balloons and floats. It's hot dogs and antique fire engines and Uncle Sam on stilts. It's 4-H kids and beauty queens and star athletes. It's politicians and community leaders and of course, soldiers in step. But even with those soldiers, the emphasis isn't on guns, though some may carry them—it's on fifes and drums and music.

And most of all, the flag.

We showcase not armor, but Americana; not our hardware, but our spirit.

In 1967, I went to the World's Fair in Montreal. I was only 14 but still noticed a clear difference between foreign exhibits and our own. The others were all displays of technology: Mini-museums of science, impressive but sterile.

Then there was America, which could have outboasted them all, only we didn't try, because technology may be where we excel, but it's not who we are. Our exhibit reflected that, focusing on matters of the heart.

There was a hall of Hollywood's nostalgia, posters of Gable and Bogey and the rest of them. Most of all I remember a documentary, the exhibit's featured movie, produced as a glimpse of America. Only there wasn't a single image of great skyscrapers, great factories or great products. It was about children at play.

And one more memory, this of our 210th July 4th parade, in 1986. It was a grand celebration, the TV coverage extensive. The highpoint has stayed with me. No, not tanks, there are never tanks. The high point was the swearing in of thousands of new citizens—citizens drawn here by our most powerful weapon. Our spirit.

I didn't enjoy that Bastille Day parade in Paris, but I'm glad I saw it. It gave me a valuable glimpse into a nation's soul.

Our own.

CONFESSIONS OF A PASSIONATE PRINCESS

A judge recently ordered Random House to pay Joan Collins $2.6 million for a novel they asked her to write, then rejected as "drivel." Its title is Passion. If bad romance writing is worth that much, it's time I tried it:

She stared hungrily at him in the stable as he saddled her steed. She whispered his name to herself, as if it were prayer, a plea, an incantation: James. James Howitt. James her magnificent riding tutor. James whose muscles rippled beneath his shirt as seductively as his blond tresses did in the breeze. How she yearned to be lost in those arms, arms skinny by normal standards but compared to those of her husband, downright robust.

Her husband. He of ears bigger than his biceps. A ponderous brooding sort. A fuddy-dud who preferred hiking in his foolish kilt in the Scottish moors to dancing the night away in London. He was late 40s, a dozen years her elder, and acted twice that. She hated him as passionately as she thirsted, ached, hungered for James.

Despised her husband, really. Loathed him. Detested, disdained, reviled and scorned him.

How did she end up with such a man?

She knew, of course. All England knew, thanks to the tabloid leeches, those rumpled, overweight ink-stained parasites who spent their days peeking through her keyhole and calling it a living.

She knew. And way back when, should have known better.

I'll make you a princess, he said. You'll have palaces, position and popularity. Not to mention alliteration. Give me an heir and a spare and I'll provide you with all you've dreamed of.

And yes, she told him, yes. And the dream began, the dream of every young girl, only with her, it had come true—the tiara, the title, the treasure, the tribute.

The trap.

That's what this gilded life had become to her: A posh prison, a palatial penitentiary, a plush pokey.

She gave him what he asked for, birthing in pain two fine young males. In return, this was his gratitude: He deserted her, emotionally anyway, that is if he'd ever been there for her to start with. On reflection, she doubted it. He had the emotions of a subway loo.

"I love you," she'd implored when she first felt the chasm widening between them.

"Quite right," he responded.

Quite right.

That was as torrid, as steamy, as wanton as he ever got. Quite right, indeed. The whole bloody family had Freon in their veins. Oh, why hadn't she trusted her instincts—her eyes. She needed only glance at his mother, the queen. A human mannequin if there ever was one. Look up "solemn" in the dictionary and you'd see the old bat's portrait.

She thought back, back to that perfect summer day in St. Paul's, the whole world watching, she looking resplendent, radiant, ravishing in her wedding dress, he so striking in his uniform that for once she did not care about his bald spot.

But how quickly it all soured. How bitter the memory of that day she arrived at Balmoral and saw . . . her. Hostessing by his side.

How could he? How could he bring that hag into their life - that trollop, that hussy, that tramp. A horse from the neck up, a dried-up tart from the neck down.

How could he prefer that to her - the world's first princess-cover girl. Didn't she work out daily in the gym? Didn't she dare to display decolletage? Didn't the Sun call her seductive? The Guardian gorgeous? The Times tantalizing? She'd like to see what the tabs would call that harlot of his.

And yet the harlot is who he preferred. Or is the right word "whom" ? Being thick as a plank upstairs, she hadn't a clue. But she did know what counted: That the marriage felt pretty crowded with three of them.

She'd tried hard to win back his attention. When the decolletage didn't work, she tried tossing herself down some stairs. Then bulimia. When that failed, she turned to inflicting pain upon her arms. Her next cry for help was spending $100,000 a year on new clothes. At last, she threw herself at his feet and cried that she'd sunk into suicidal despondency.

She'd never forget his response. "Chin up," he said as he stepped over her and then out the door, polo mallet in hand.

Who could blame her for feeling starved, ravenous, voracious for the company of another man? Who? Or was it "whom"?

And then she met Howitt. Her riding tutor. Her fantasy.

He had the chiseled face of a Greek god and the kind of shallow mind that mirrored her own. He was her golden-maned dream. Her destiny.

She was spellbound, bewitched, captivated, mesmerized. How, she thought, could she live without him? Or for that matter, without a thesaurus?

As he touched her hand, the world spun before her. She felt herself drawn to him as are filings to a 10-pound magnet.

She closed her eyes and waited for the hot press of his lips against her.

Instead, shockingly, she heard the scratch of a Bic pen against parchment.

"What are you doing?" she asked.

"Taking notes for my tell-all book about our tryst," he said. I'm thinking of calling it either 'Hot Royal Mama' or 'A Princess in Love.' "

Could she trust no one? It was at that moment that she remembered a wise saying: A woman first needs looks, then a husband, at last money. She had come to "at last" sooner than she expected, but here she was.

A year later, after both she and the prince had each told their sides of the story first through books, then BBC interviews, the palace offered her $21 million as a divorce settlement.

She met the prince privately and told him she'd take not a shilling under $45 million.

"Forty-five?" he sputtered, aghast, shocked, panicked and petrified.

She smiled that coy world-renowned smile of hers, only this time with a devilish twist at the corners of her ruby-red lips.

"Quite right," she spat. "Quite right."

(The above are fictional characters. Any similarities to real people are strictly the fault of readers who spend too much time perusing supermarket tabloids. I await my check from Random House, and will hire Joan Collins's lawyer if I don't get it.)

🕐

THE LORD'S WORK

A fellow congregant called her at home just after 5 a.m. There's a fire at the synagogue, he said.

The synagogue's name was Beth David, located in a Boston suburb named Westwood. Marcia Ringel, the president, got in her car. She was hoping it would be a small fire, but as she got closer, she could see the flames coming over the trees. She arrived just in time to see the roof cave in.

At noon, the fire chief told her what he'd found. They'd checked the wiring, the furnace, the kitchen—everything—and all were normal. Someone had broken inside, piled up papers and boxes, and set the temple on fire.

But this is not a story about arson alone. It's a story about America. To tell it right, it's important to first tell of how people in another community react to the burning of holy places. It's a common occurrence in Northern Ireland. I spent several weeks there one spring.

In Belfast, I visited the remains of St. Enoch's, once the biggest Presbyterian church in all Ireland. Because it was on the line of a Catholic ghetto, someone set it on fire. They did it by piling pew cushions on gas heaters. Eventually, the gas exploded. St. Enoch's had been there 100 years, it even survived the bombs of World War II. It did not survive the bigotry of an unknown neighbor. The community's reaction: Few came forward to help rebuild, no one of other faiths. St. Enoch's remains a shell.

I explored a similar incident in the town of Limavady. A Catholic congregation there had just finished building a new church. The cornerstone had been dedicated by John Paul II, which made it particularly sacred. Just before it was to open, Protestant extremists placed a bomb inside it. It destroyed the church.

How did the community react? I found out from a liberal Protestant minister named David Armstrong who'd just arrived in town as the pastor of that church. When I talked with him about it, he was not sure what disturbed him the most, the bombing itself, or the phone calls he got afterward.

"What right did they have to build there in the first place?" said one caller.

"I'm delighted," said another.

"It's a pity they weren't worshipping there when the roof came down," said a third.

Westwood, Mass., has a very small Jewish population. Marcia Ringel estimates it at only a few percent. Many of the temple's 140 families, she said, come from nearby towns. But on the morning of the fire, she was surprised at who were among the first people to come by: The community's ministers and priests. For much of the morning, they stood by the rabbi, just to show their support.

As news of the fire got around, the stream of neighbors became nonstop. We're here, they told Mrs. Ringel. We'll help you find who did this. We'll help you rebuild.

I asked her if most who came by were Jewish.

No, most were non-Jews, many of them people she didn't know.

Westwood has an Interfaith Council made up of the town's clergy. Two days after the fire, it called an open meeting to talk about what was to become of Beth David. So many people showed up they could not all get into the auditorium. Before the night was over, they raised $3,700.

One of the hard rules in Northern Ireland is that you don't go into the other religion's holy places. The young Protestant minister I spoke with in Limavady made the mistake of doing so. After the town's Catholics rebuilt their church, he went inside to help them celebrate the opening. Afterward, his own congregation vilified him as a traitor, ultimately firing him.

Compare that with Westwood: The temple there burned on the Jewish holiday of Purim. That night, the local Baptist church invited the congregation to have services in its hall. Since then, every church in town has opened its doors. The past few weeks, the people of Beth David have been holding their Friday Sabbath services in St. Margaret Mary's Catholic church.

The fire irreparably scorched Beth David's torah scrolls. One had been considered a special treasure. It was from Czechoslovakia, and had survived the Holocaust. It is Jewish tradition to show respect to damaged holy books by burying them. The congregation organized a procession to the cemetery. It was led by two Westwood fire department cars. The fire chief, John Sheehy, who was raised Catholic, was in one of the cars.

"We wanted to show concern for our neighbors," he said.

It was estimated that it will cost more than $800,000 to rebuild Beth David, and the insurance will only pay for a small part of it. But within weeks, non-Jewish neighbors had contributed more than $30,000. On some days, said Mrs. Ringel, more than 100 checks came in. The town Rotary club announced a fundraiser for the temple. Students in the junior high school ran a bake sale for it, and car wash.

I spoke with Mrs. Ringel's husband, too. "The way this community has reached out," he said, "would make you cry."

Many in Northern Ireland kept telling me how lucky we are in this country. We don't know how deeply religions hate each other in much of the world. We don't know the uniqueness of our tradition of tolerance, and coexistence. We don't know.

A temple was set on fire in Westwood, Mass.

It was a story of arson.

And a story of America.

I ADMIT IT, I DID IT

Confessions:

■ When I'm a guest at people's houses, I've been known to look in their medicine cabinets.

■ I call directory assistance even if there's a phone book nearby.

■ When my wife's not looking, I sneak sweet and sour sauce into her stew.

■ In 1971, while trying to impress Jane Brown by riding a horse bareback, I fell off and broke my right wrist in two places.

■ I let my dog lick me on the mouth.

■ I read the National Enquirer while standing in the grocery line. Sometimes even Weekly World News.

■ On the highway, I feel smug when I pass a monster traffic jam going the other way.

■ In high school, I made penciled flip movies in the margins of my textbooks. Okay, college, too.

■ I sometimes climb into the kitchen garbage can and jump up and down to compact the trash.

■ I cannot sleep without a huggy pillow.

■ My father hasn't gotten my name right on the first try in 10 years.

■ I own approximately 120 ties, but wear only three.

■ When women touch my upper arms, I secretly flex.

■ Up until age 15, when served Brussels sprouts for dinner, I'd slip them into my pant cuffs, ask to go to the bathroom and flush them away.

■ I once put a $500 dent in my father's car while trying to park it, then told him a hit-and-run driver sideswiped me.

■ I avoided grammar school over a dozen times by holding a thermometer against a hot light bulb.

■ My best golf score is over 125.

■ At age 12, I stole a nylon stocking out of my mother's dresser and wore it over my head at night to "train" my hair.

■ I spent endless hours as a youth teaching myself to squirt a perfect stream of water between my two front teeth, hitting targets up to five feet away.

■ Okay, I still practice that.

■ Two or three times a week, I fantasize about rescuing my wife from motorcycle gangs.

■ Ultimate confession: This column should be longer, but there are a few I can't own up to for the sake of domestic tranquillity.

■ All right—just one: When alone in the kitchen after being assigned to sponge the crumbs off the table, I brush them into a pile, make sure the coast is clear, then whisk them into midair.

■ But I won't confirm that I kick dropped pieces of ice under the refrigerator...

■ And I swear it wasn't me who's been putting those empty cereal boxes in the cupboard because walking four steps to throw them out is too difficult...

■ ...And I have no idea who used staples to hold my shirt cuff together after the button fell off...

■ And you know what? Confession may be good for a man's soul, but as far as his marriage, I need to give that one some more thought.

THE BENEFIT OF BRUSQUENESS

He **was eating at the counter,** a thin cane by his side. The restaurant was crowded, and I had to wait by the cash register for a table. He was alone, and it made me wonder how such a young man manages.

I watched as he picked up his cane and began moving slowly toward the cash register. A number of people saw him and moved out of the way, but some didn't, and it was clear he was going to run into someone in a moment. I decided to get past my reserve and reach out to help.

As he passed me, I grasped him by the arm and began to say, "Excuse me." But before I'd gotten out the phrase, he turned his face my way and spoke in a near shout, plenty loud enough for everyone in the restaurant to hear.

"Take your hands off me."

For a moment, the whole place fell silent.

"I was just trying to help," I finally said. He answered in a voice still angry.

"Then why didn't you ask?"

Then he paid his bill and was gone.

A half-hour later, as I paid for my own lunch, I noticed a notecard pinned to the restaurant's bulletin board. It was from a blind graduate student requesting help in reading mail and books. The name on the card was Charles. The cashier told me it was the same young man. I wrote down the phone number, and when I got home, I called him.

The voice that answered was the same, though more pleasant. I told him I'd seen his request on the restaurant wall. "But that's not why I'm calling. There's something else I wondered if I could ask you about."

"Yes?"

"Well, I'm the guy you just yelled at in the restaurant, and I'm trying to understand what I did wrong."

I waited a beat. So did he.

"Well, thank you so much," he finally said. "Most people think I'm the one who did something rude—they tell me to go to hell all the time. So I thank you for being sensitive enough to know that you're the one with a problem."

He was direct, I'll give him that.

"I was just trying to let you know you were an inch from a collision," I said.

"That's what the cane is for," he told me. "It's terribly offensive to just grab someone." He said it happens many times a day. I asked if he always reacts the same.

"I didn't used to," he said. "I used to be more polite. But after years of that kind of thing, you get fed up."

I asked if he thought most sightless people feel the same way.

He explained there are three categories. The first, like him, feel offended and say so. The second feel the same, but act polite.

"The third category welcomes it," he said. "That's the kind of person who's been trained into being a blind person and fits it. They believe that because they're blind, they're helpless and deserving of pity."

He'll be 30 in October. He's going for a doctorate in philosophy at Brown University and hopes one day to teach. As we talked, I kept using the word "sightless." He finally stopped me.

"You can use the word 'blind,' " he said. "Saying things like 'sightless,' or 'how long have you been this way,' just implies that blindness is such a terrible tragedy that you—the blind person—can't cope with the word. So everyone pussyfoots around."

I told him I still didn't understand why he wouldn't welcome those who want to give him a hand.

"I never reject a simple, 'Excuse me, may I help you,' " he said. "But what's offensive is people just grabbing you. Or suddenly shouting: 'Go to your right. Go to your left.' People think that because you're blind, you're also deaf."

Does he prefer moving through the city on his own?

"Ideally," he said, "it would make things easier to always have someone at my side. But where am I going to find that person? Since I'm a busy person, since I want to do things, I have to get around by my self."

Does he ever ask for help on his own?

"Sure," he said. "I know the help I need and the help I don't, and I take responsibility for asking for it. That's the issue. Who has the control?"

I mentioned to him that I was a journalist. Would it be all right to do a story on our talk? I promised to leave out his name. He insisted I used it—Charles Guttman.

"You have a pretty tough shell," I told him.

"I have a right to feel that way," he said. "I've been pushed around too many times."

If you ask me, I still think he's too brusque to strangers with good intentions. But perhaps we occasionally need brusque souls to make us understand. Now, I do.

🕐

GETTING TO KNOW ME PROBABLY ISN'T WORTH THE ENCOUNTER INVOLVED

I got in the mood for some nostalgia the other night and decided to watch "Bob & Carol & Ted & Alice." It's about two 40ish California couples trying to get in touch with themselves. Now that we're in the midst of a more materialistic time, I wanted to remember the more meaningful 1970s.

The first scene showed Bob and Carol at a group encounter session. They were told to walk up to the other participants and just stare in silence. Look right into their souls, the leader said. And give. Give of yourselves. Not for a few seconds, but for long, meaningful minutes.

Personally, I get embarrassed staring at my dog in silence, let alone strangers. That scene, and the rest of the movie, taught me something I'd never before really thought about.

Am I glad the 70s are over.

I was never good at the 70s. I'm now 43 and still haven't figured out how to get in touch with my feelings, which is all folks did that decade.

There are two kinds of people in this world. First, those who ask you how you feel, and when you say fine, they take your forearm, look at you with concern and say, "How do you really feel?"

Then there are the people who can't even say the L-word to their own mothers, as in "I l--- you, mom." I'm in that category. That's why the 70s were a bad time for me. No one was allowed to just talk, you had to interact meaningfully. You couldn't just do things, you had to experience them. Simple exercise wasn't even enough for physical toning, you had to get Rolfed in order to realign body segments with gravity and release blocked energy.

The worst part was the fad therapies. I was never comfortable with the idea of prolonged transformational processes where you spend a weekend locked in a room with 30 strangers being coaxed by an EST leader into spontaneously realizing that what is, is. Or that the main thing is to feel what you feel.

My biggest fear in the 70s was that I'd be asked to go through rebirthing, wherein one eliminates the neuroses of adulthood by redoing it the right way. The right way involved first donning a snorkel and being immersed in 99-degree water to simulate the womb. Eventually, you emerged naked into the air where you were gently massaged and "welcomed" by strangers, thereby undoing the psychic damage caused by the trauma of your real birth. Personally, I think real birth is less embarrassing.

I'm not saying those things were wrong. It's just that I don't do well at psychic sharing.

"I think we're getting close to the root of your neuroses," the therapist says. "If you could just help me with the main childhood trauma that left you emotionally stunted."

"Not your business," I would answer.

I'd be worse in group therapy.

"I think it's time we talk about you, Mark," the leader would say. "Why do you think you seem to have so much hostility toward the group?"

"For me to know and you to find out."

"That was beautiful. Thank you for sharing such honesty. I feel closer to you now."

All of this is one reason why I get along so well with my wife. She is as emotionally reserved as I am. Her way of expressing affection is to say, "This marriage could be a lot lousier, you know."

To which I respond: "You're not the ugliest woman I've ever had dinner with." It works for us. It was that side of her that first made me think it could be serious: I realized early on that she was un-70s.

"You seem distant," I once said to her. "Anything wrong?"

"I hate that part," she said.

"What part?"

"The part of dating where you have to discuss how you feel about the relationship."

"You mean where it's impossible to just be in a quiet mood, because the other person will take it personally?"

"Yes," she said. "That part."

"I hate that part, too,"

After watching "Bob & Carol & Ted & Alice," she was also glad the 70s were over. I'll bet most of you think the same. The test is how you react to what I'm about to say:

I don't want to know how you think about the 70s. Share with me how you feel. How you really feel.

🕐

AN ODE TO TOUGH BOSSES

I **just saw another** "How-To-Manage" article saying it's better to be a nice boss than a tough one. As an employee, I at first agreed. Then I got to thinking about which bosses I've learned the most from.

The first, Wayne Brasler, wasn't technically a boss, he was a teacher, but he ran my high school newspaper, which I worked on, so it was close.

One week, I finished an article a day late. Because this was also a journalism class assignment, my story was part of my grade. Mr. Brasler read it carefully. "One of the best things you've ever written," he said. Then, without looking up: "I'm giving you an 'F'."

It was my first F. I'd gotten a few D's, but never an F. Looking at that big circled red letter was shocking.

"But you said it was good."

"You missed your deadline," Mr. Brasler said. "You can't do that in journalism."

Did I get angry. That's unfair, I said—the paper didn't go to press until the next morning. The article would make it in plenty of time.

"You still missed your assigned deadline. It was yesterday. F."

Mr. Brasler was usually the funnest teacher in the school. This was out of character. How could he be so suddenly inflexible? What was on his mind?

Today, I know what. It was one of the best things he ever did for me. I still occasionally push deadlines, but if it weren't for that F, I'd be far worse. A lesson that harsh sticks.

My first job out of college was on a newspaper in Utica, N.Y. The top editor was Gil Smith, a serious, fatherly figure. I thought I was hot stuff. I thought I was too good for minor assignments, like rewriting press releases. I did them, but hurriedly. Then one day, while doing a short blurb on a Rotary Club luncheon, I mixed up the names of the club president and the guest speaker.

We printed it that way. A junior editor brought it to my attention with some amusement and said we needed to do a correction. I was amused, too—what was the harm; it was only a Rotary lunch.

Then I felt a tap on my shoulder. Gil Smith. Not a word, he just motioned me into his office. He asked if I realized what I'd done. I admitted I'd made a mistake, but told Mr. Smith that at least it was minor.

His eyes narrowed. "Listen to me, young man. Most business-people in town are going to that lunch, and a 'minor' mistake like that tells them we don't know what we're doing."

What he said next almost made me start crying: "Around here, we warn them once, then we fire 'em. I'm warning you once."

That night, I called my mother to tell her what a mean, unfair man I worked for and maybe I should apply somewhere else. But he wasn't mean. He just knew that when you're a boss, being nice or fatherly is fine most of the time, but not always. I've made a few other mistakes since then, but far fewer than had Mr. Smith failed to warn me once—and never because I thought a story was so minor it didn't matter.

Al Johnson was my first boss at the paper I work for now, the Providence Journal. He used to be night city editor. For two years, I was terrified of the man, partly because I thought he kept hanging up on me from exasperation when I'd call from the field. "What do you have?" he'd say. Then: "When will you have it?" As soon as I answered: click. Only later did someone tell me he wasn't hanging up at all, he was just so busy he didn't have time to say goodbye. Also, he wasn't the chatty kind.

A few times, I'd come up to him in the city room after some assignment, and start my conversation with what I thought to be some funny story about my night, but he'd cut me off. "Never mind that. What do you have? When will you have it?"

In time, I found he was basically shy, even a sweetheart—a label he probably wouldn't love, but sorry, Mr. Johnson, it's accurate, another thing you always stressed.

Nevertheless, he was tough in that chair, feeling his job was to get you to do assignments quick and right, rather than being your counselor.

Finally, there was Jack Monaghan. He was my first column editor. When he didn't like something I wrote, he wasn't real diplomatic. "This is rat-dirt, kid," he'd say. Actually, I cleaned up his language a bit. Today, now that I've been at it a while, I'm not sure I'd take a line like that as gracefully. And it didn't help my ego then. But when you're fresh meat on the job, and you drop the ball, it helps in the long run to be told it straight.

Of course, this is the '90s and bosses are supposed to be your friend. Like I said, no argument there.

But when I look back, it sure is interesting what lessons stuck with me most.

MODERN MEDICINE LEAVES ME WITH A HOLLOW FEELING

Until recently, there was no way to diagnose sports injuries with precision. You'd go to the doctor, who'd bend your arm and ask whether it hurt, and after you were revived, and confirmed that it did, he'd always give you the same verdict. "Looks like a strain," he'd say.

Luckily, we're now in a much more progressive age. We have MRI.

This stands for Magnetic Resonance Imaging, something out of the year 2001 that takes detailed pictures of the inside of your body, section by section, as clear as slices of deli roast beef, not that medical people would ever use so insensitive a phrase.

Anyway, having suffered a still-painful sports injury to my elbow four months ago, I decided to go high-tech and get an MRI. It's one of the most impressive pieces of equipment I've ever seen—a half dozen video screens, a thousand dials. I'm in awe of anyone who can operate it. It looks almost as hard as setting the time on a VCR.

I asked one of the technicians just how clear a picture of my arm they could get. "Clear as slices of deli roast beef," she said.

Then they told me the drill: I'd have to lie down on a stretcher-like platform and be slid inside a long, narrow tube. I would be in there about 30 minutes. It looked painless, even restful. Maybe, I thought, I could doze. I lay down on my stomach and got comfortable. That lasted a good five seconds.

Then they cranked my bad arm forward and locked it into place. They cranked my other arm against my leg and strapped that down. Finally, they jammed cushions up and down my body, alleging it was to make me snug and relaxed. I didn't want to be impolite, so I thanked them, which was akin to thanking the Iraqi security police for putting you in a hammerlock.

At last, they asked if I was claustrophobic, the kind of question men love, because then we can say, "no problem," and feel rugged.

"No problem," I said. A moment later, I was inside the tube, and it helped me gain an insight about myself I'd never known before. I'm not ugged; I'm claustrophobic. Though I think a mole would be claustrophobic n an MRI tube. Picture a dolphin in a golf bag.

"All right," said one of the techs, "the first phase will last three minutes." And I had to be absolutely still: move nothing.

You cannot know how long three minutes is until you spend it in a unning MRI machine. I don't know who designed these things, but I'd like o ask them why they sealed midget construction workers with ackhammers inside the tube. That's how loud it is.

"The next phase will last four minutes."

This is where I came to my first theory about MRI. Have you ever vondered what happened to the East Germans who made their livings extracting information from suspects before communism collapsed? I'm iow convinced they sneaked into America and became MRI operators. Iad I been a spy, I'd have talked.

"Next phase. Five minutes this time."

Lying there, I began to picture the first lecture MRI techs are given in raining. "Ladies and gentlemen," says the professor, "remember our most basic philosophy: The treatment must be more traumatic than the illness."

"Stay still again, this time for six minutes."

"Thank you very much," I said, trying to ingratiate myself to my ntagonists. I think they call that the Swedish hostage syndrome.

Then they turned on a fan, again alleging it was only to make me more omfortable. But I soon got cold, and colder, and then it hit me. This vhole MRI thing is an elaborate scam. The idea is to lure innocent patients ito a tube, where their bodies are frozen and their organs later harvested or sale on the black market.

Luckily, the week I went, the organs market must have been slow. hey let me out in one piece. They sent me on my way with my 21st-entury pictures.

A day later, I stood by my doctor while he put my MRI shots against iewing lights. They were indeed extraordinary. He nodded solemnly. I was bout to get my futuristic diagnosis.

"Looks like a strain," he said.

THE PRICE YOU'LL PAY

This is for you who've lived on the netherside of crime, you who think prison is worth the risk. It's for you who break into houses, and into lives, and have the potential to do worse. It's for you who think: If they catch you, well, prison is an acceptable risk. You can do prison.

But did you happen to read about him?

Did you happen to see how badly he wants to get out? How well he combs his hair before he meets with the parole board? How desperately he pleads? Did you see how he'll promise anything, if only they give him his freedom?

You who think you can do prison, take a moment to consider him. Consider Sirhan Sirhan, a name you perhaps have not heard mentioned in while. That happens to those we incarcerate; the world forgets them. They disappear. They become nothing. But they are still there, of course, languishing

As you could be.

He has been forced to spend the most promising years of his manhood in a cage. He went into Soledad, in California, while almost a youth, 24; now he is middle-aged, over 50. Every two years, he is allowed to come before the parole board. Each time, he appears increasingly desperate with regret. Time has brought him to understand a secret only caged men can truly know: Nothing is worth this risk.

Have you read about how fervently he pleads at his hearings? He feels endless remorse, he tells the board. Every day he laments the death of Robert Kennedy. Please, Sirhan tells them—if they gave him his freedom, he would live in peace, in obedience, just as he has in prison. He would agree to be deported—do anything, vow any vow if only they would let him out.

They haven't, despite nine pleadings. And that's the other secret. They don't always let you out.

But this isn't being written for him, it's for you, on the netherside of crime. Can you picture what it will be like? Do you know how small a cell s? Smaller than a dorm room, and almost always with another person in the bunk above you. There is no privacy—no separate bathroom, no door to close, just bars. You live 12 to 14 hours a day like that, with your keepers watching. Can you picture the absence of freedom? No restaurants to eat in, no cars to drive, no chance to lie on the beach and let your body brown in the sun. And where will you run if someone too strong for you, someone who's been without a woman for 10 years, decides to make you his boy? You've heard about that, haven't you? About how newcomers become a certain kind of prey? Can you do that kind of prison?

I've interviewed several inmates before. I still remember what one of them told me.

"What kind of day is a good day in here?" I asked.

"You never have a good day in here," he said.

When I was done with that interview, two guards told the prisoner to come with them; he would have to be strip-searched. He got angry, cussing first at them, then at me. He said he would never have agreed to an interview had he known this would happen. You'll do what you're told, the guards said. That is prison. Every hour of every day, you do only what you're told.

It is said that the absence of freedom can cause physical pain. Read about Sirhan, and you'll know how deeply he aches. He has lost his youth, and today, every day, he is terrified that he'll lose his middle age, too; that he'll suddenly wake up with his hair white, and his skin wrinkled like the neck of a turtle, and still the bars will be there.

He is right to be so afraid. Does he know that we've not even begun to make him pay? These 28 years he's served, these 10,000 mornings—does he know he may not even be at the halfway point yet? Keep counting, Sirhan. Count as the next 10,000 mornings of your life come and go, in your cage.

His final plea would doubtless be your own: Yes, he did it, but he was young. Wild. Drunk. It was an angry, aberrant moment. He is a different person, now. He's not a monster. Nothing like it could ever happen again.

You who break into houses and into lives, you who feel you'll always be forgiven for your youth, your wildness, your alcohol—know this: We will make you pay even for aberrant moments. We will make you pay more dearly than you think possible.

Perhaps you still think you can abide such a price. But I saw a photograph of Sirhan recently. I looked at it close. I think, there in his cage, his hair has begun to turn gray. I look forward to seeing it turn white

🕐

WHEN MORE IS LESS, EARLY IS LATE, AND OTHER TRUISMS OF LIFE

Laws Of Life:

- The fancier the restaurant, the smaller the portion.

- Dropped toast always lands butter-side down.

- Never trust a man who wears sunglasses indoors.

- The more inconsequential the agenda, the longer the meeting.

- If you're late for a plane, it will leave on time; if you miss it and reschedule on the next flight, that one will be postponed.

- The greater the hype, the worse the movie.

- Or at least the more expensive it was to make.

- How to find a misplaced item within 24 hours: Buy a replacement.

- The more important it is for you to get sleep in a hotel, the more likely the person next door will be hard of hearing and into Letterman.

- Never give your Social Security check to TV ministers whose wives wear too much eye makeup.

- The farther a man lives from his office, the more important his job.

- The three most dangerous words spoken on a ski slope: "Follow me, Dad."

- The more unpleasant the contents of the Hefty bag you've set on the curb, the more likely a band of famished Dobermans will find it.

- The view of Niagara Falls is always out the other side of the plane.

- He who shouts first loses the argument.

- The chance of a public address system breaking down increases in proportion to the nervousness of the speaker.

- If a plate can't be washed in a dishwasher, or heated in a microwave, don't buy it.

- If it has to be ironed, don't buy that, either.

■ The more frantically you rush to grab a ringing phone, the more likely they'll hang up just as you say hello.

■ People who have a "III" after their name act the part.

■ Never buy a used car if the radio buttons are all on hard rock stations.

■ Be wary of executives who have their secretary place phone calls fo them.

■ Magazine subscription mailings that say "LAST CHANCE" really mean you'll get five more.

■ The more full your mouth is at a restaurant, the more likely a waitresses will ask if everything's all right.

■ Forgetting to save data on your computer increases the chance of a power outage.

■ The more important your "To Do" list, the more likely it will be put through the wash.

■ In exotic countries, always agree with soldiers carrying machine guns.

■ The more important the job interview, the more likely you'll forget that piece of Kleenex you placed on a shaving cut.

■ The grocery line you choose will always be the slowest.

■ When the phone company says the repairman will be there between noon and 5, it will be 4:59.

■ The heavier your carry-on luggage, the farther the departure gate.

■ If you drop car keys, there is a 40-percent chance you are standing on a sewer grate.

■ You never discover the spoon in your garbage disposal until you've turned it on.

■ Washing machines only break during the wash cycle, never the spin.

■ The once a month you go to McDonald's because you're hurried, a high school field trip will be at the counter.

■ Objects dropped on the floor will roll to a room's most inaccessible corner; even square ones.

■ The more meaningless the assignment, the more your boss will ride you on it.

■ You pay for everything.

■ The later you are for an appointment, the more red lights you'll hit en route.

■ Cars never break down until the warranty expires; actually, nothing does.

■ No matter how much money you have, it's never enough.

■ The later you are, the greater the chance the lights will be red.

■ Bills left on desks mate.

■ The grocery bag that breaks is always the one with the glass jars.

■ The chance of dripping gravy on your shirt is in direct proportion to the importance of the person you're dining with.

■ Type B drivers are always ahead of Type A drivers.

■ Furnaces only break down on Saturday nights. In February.

■ Pens left on countertops evaporate.

■ The more you hate cats, the more they will be drawn to your lap.

■ If there are two must-watch shows on television you have to see during the week, they will be at the same hour on different channels.

■ Women only go into labor after midnight.

■ The plow always pushes the snow into the driveways on your side of the street.

■ Any movie with the number 3 after the title will be mediocre at best.

■ Whenever a writer makes an embarrassing misspelling, the copy editor will miss it.

■ The closer you are to deadline, the harder it is to think of the last line of a column.

A LIFE COMPLICATED BY ELLIPSES

We headed for his favorite restaurant, soon spotting the arches up ahead. He ordered a hot fudge sundae, an 11-year-old boy's idea of the perfect dinner. Then he told me he'd have to be up late with his homework when he got back. I asked why.

"I missed yesterday because of court again," he said. "Custody and all."

His mother had agreed to let the two of us talk on our own. I asked whether it had been his first time in court.

"No. It's been postponed five or six times. And I miss school every time. It's like you go down for nothing."

I stirred a sugar into my coffee and asked why there had to be a hearing.

"Well, my father thinks it would be better to live up there with him."

Up there, he said, is eight hours by car. His father now gets him every other weekend, every other holiday and every other vacation. With his mother, he's an only child. With his father, there's a half brother and half sister.

He finished his sundae. I asked if he wanted another.

"No thank you."

"My newspaper can afford it."

"Okay."

He returned from the counter and began spooning the fudge first. As he ate, I told him the court fight at least means both his parents love him.

"I don't know," he said. "Sometimes my dad treats me like a possession. It's like he has to win."

How did he mean that?

"A lot of times, he'll give me a toy or something, and promise to take me places if I stay, but if I say I want to go back home, he won't."

I asked if he thought most kids understand the difference between a parent who's being nice and one who's trying to buy them.

"Probably not," he said. "Not if they're below 10 or something."

Has he had a chance to testify?

"Not to the judge, but they gave me a court guardian. Though I think he takes my father's side because he's going through a divorce too."

"Has anyone just sat you down and asked what you want?"

"Not yet. You need the custody hearing for that. But supposedly I get to say so when I finally get on the chair or whatever it is."

He told me his favorite sports are soccer and deck tennis. His favorite music is rock 'n' roll. I asked if he thought he was too young to be in the middle of this. He scraped the bottom of the sundae cup as he answered.

"If this is what my childhood is going to be like, then I don't want to see my adulthood. I'll say that."

"What's your dad do for a living?"

"A doctor."

I asked him what he wants to be himself.

"Maybe a lawyer."

"Why?"

"Money."

I laughed.

"Let's be real," he said, smiling. "Your newspaper doesn't publish just to inform folks. They do it for money."

I asked if his parents ever tell him critical things about each other.

"They're not allowed."

"Not allowed?"

"There's a court order that says they can't."

"They issue court orders like that?"

"Yep. I think it's a good decree. But my father still tells me my mother has a negative attitude and stuff."

We talked some more about how the court process works. He explained that the judge will decide who gets him.

"Isn't there an age when you get to decide yourself?"

"Yeah, 13 I think. Or 12. I hope it's 12."

I asked if he had any advice for other kids who find themselves facing this.

"Yeah. Know what you want and say it. And not to turn into a grouch or take a grumpy pill if things don't look so good."

We began to put our coats on. I asked how often he thinks about the custody battle.

"All the time," he said. "When I'm with my father, it's like, will the plane be canceled? Will I ever go home? Will my mother die? What will the court say? Lots of ellipses."

I asked what ellipses are.

"The three dots."

And what does he think will happen when the judge finally rules?

"Life isn't like TV," he said. "The good guys don't always win."

He finished his sundae. I drove him home in the dark.

🕓

MY CUP OF JOE HAS AN IDENTITY CRISIS

For **most of my adult life,** it was easy to know what to order when I walked into a coffee shop. Coffee. I'm afraid so simple a time in America is gone.

Over the past months, I've begun to visit '90s coffee places, and I've found you no longer can get away with saying "light with one sugar, please." Things have gotten much more complicated.

By the way, I use the phrase, coffee "places" because coffee "shop" is passé. Sounds too much like where you get a cup of burnt Maxwell House at a roadside motel. At such coffee shops, there was usually one entry on the coffee portion of the menu. Coffee.

At coffee places, menus now have four pages with dozens of coffee options. I have here a typical menu from such a '90s shop—the California Coffee Company, aptly named because the West Coast is where they invent all new gastronomic trends. They didn't come up with goat cheese pizza in Dubuque.

This being an establishment dedicated to coffee, you'd expect the first offering at the top of the menu to be just that, coffee. It's not. It's Espresso. That's super-strong coffee along the lines of Number-6 crude oil. The Europeans have been drinking it for years, which is one reason no one gets along over there. They're too jittery.

Then the options get more elaborate. You can also get cappuccino. That's a shot of espresso mixed with 1/3 steamed milk and 1/3 milk foam. It's a curious concept: First make coffee super-strong to distinguish it from normal coffee, then mix it with enough milk to make it taste like normal coffee again.

But I'm afraid if all you ordered was a cappuccino, no one would be impressed. Cappuccino has been around a while. To be really hip, you have to at least order a latte: That's a shot of espresso and also...I forget what else, but it's hipper than cappuccino. Actually, I think it's cappuccino without the foam, advantageous since anyone who's drunk cappuccino knows that each sip gives you a milk mustache that goes to your eyebrows.

If you do order a latte, you have to know how to pronounce it. It's "Lot-TAY." The first time I ordered it, I asked for a "laddie." This earned me condescending looks from the 19-year-olds with nose-rings who run the counters at most coffee places. If you want to get hired to serve latte, get your nose pierced, it's a job requirement.

Anyway, once you get the pronunciation down, things get more complicated still. It's not enough to just say, "Latte please." You will then be asked, "Cinnamon or chocolate?" Those are sprinkled toppings.

But we haven't even begun to talk complexity. There are also myriad offerings with names like Espresso Macchiato—espresso topped with foam. I think it's federal law that you have to give these new coffee drinks foreign names. Of the scores I've seen on coffee place menus, I haven't once come across a Cappuccino Ethel or Espresso Herbert.

Anyway, you need to get all the way to page three of most menus before you at last find a listing for simple . . . coffee. Only no one calls it just "coffee" anymore. They call it "Coffee of the Day." And they indeed change it daily with exotic blends, none of which come from a Maxwell House can.

Another thing that makes the new coffee culture complex is that no one uses terms like "large" or "small". It's Grande and Short. As in: ``May I please have a short cap double shot."

And I'm also told it's not coffee culture; it's "cafe" culture.

Don't even try to master this culture, because they keep inventing new offerings each week. The latest one I spotted: A "Cafe Va"—double Espresso with Anisette Sugar, Steamed Milk and whipped cream. Sounds kind of good, actually. Many of the new concoctions do.

But you know what? Sometimes, I wish I could just stop by a roadside motel and get me a nice familiar cup of burnt Maxwell House.

A STORY WORTH TELLING

The receptionist said a young man was here to see me. It happens often at newspapers; people arrive with a story to tell but no appointment.

"Could you tell him I'm busy," I said. "And next time to please call."

"He says it's really important. Do you think you could just talk to the guy?"

The young man had dark hair, dark eyes and a sports jacket over a knit shirt. He was very polite in the way of foreigners.

"Hello Mr. Mark Patinkin," he said. "I must talk to you for an article in the newspaper. Just 15 minutes."

I told him it was a bad day for me.

"Please," he said. "Five minutes."

I could tell it had taken courage for him to come into a newsroom.

"All right. But I'm sort of on a deadline. What can I do for you?"

"My name is Abraham Malko. I come to America from Syria. I am 20 years old. When I came to this country, I couldn't speak English at all. And I found job in a pizza parlor, and I started to work hard."

I asked him to please get to the point of his story.

"My mother is very sick in hospital in Syria," he said. "I'd like small article, and picture in newspaper, so I can send to her."

What did he want the article to be about?

"I promised her I would be something in America," he said. "I'd like article, and picture, to show that Abraham has become something."

I told him newspapers can't print stories about anyone who asks. There has to be a reason.

"She's very sick," he said. "I'll pay anything you want."

He looked down for a moment.

"Why don't you just write her a letter?"

"Because if it's in newspaper," he said, "it will show her I have done something important for my life. I want her to know I have become something in America."

I didn't know how else to get rid of him, so I said we could talk. But I couldn't promise anything.

When did he come over?

"When I was seventeen and half. I found job in pizza place. I used to clean in the beginning because I couldn't speak English. After a while, I decided to learn English, and how to make pizza, and now I'm manager."

How did he learn the language?

"I would talk to people," he said. "And I would write everything I hear. And I would come back home and look it up in dictionary."

Before speaking, he would concentrate earnestly, thinking through the words. He had some papers with him and rolled them in his hands as he spoke.

"But after while," he said, "I used to look at students with books in their hands and felt guilty. How come I don't learn like others? So I decided from my heart, to study hard, and get what I want. A diploma."

So what did you do?

I went to high school. I went from 8:30 until 2 like others, like the Americans. And I work from 4:30 until 12 at night. Then I study from 12 to 2. And wake up six o'clock every day."

"When did you get your diploma?"

"In summer," he said. "All the people gave me standing ovation. Even the teachers stood. I was never happy in my life like that day."

He said he keeps his diploma on the wall of his home.

"I hope some day to repay my teachers," he said. "When I open my own restaurant, the first day, I will invite all of them for free."

That's his goal? A restaurant?

"Yes. Of course. But first I will go to college."

I asked if there was anything else he'd like his parents to know. He thought again, earnestly.

"That I live by myself. That I pay own rent, I bought car. And that nobody helped me."

I looked at the clock. Now that I had a new story to write, I really was against deadline. I told him I had no more time and walked him to the door. He turned before he left and kept thanking me. Then he asked a final question.

"Now," he said, "how much this story cost?"

I told him nothing. I was honored to be able to tell it.

A LESSON LEARNED

At first, it seemed the easiest of moral dilemmas. I'd stopped with my 2-year-old son at a drug store, then turned to check on him at a stoplight 15 minutes later and noticed a Tootsie Pop in his hand. I had not bought this Tootsie Pop. He'd obviously grabbed it from the candy rack on the way out.

But we were almost home. It probably cost a nickel. And it was hardly larceny. This was a 2-year-old. He had no idea what he'd done. It didn't make sense to kill a half hour driving back and forth over a nickel item taken in innocence.

I decided to handle it the obvious way: I explained how it's not allowed to take things from stores. Only daddies and mommies can do that. And they always have to give the lady or man money first. Always, always, always. It's very bad to take without paying.

"Okay, sport?"

"Okay, dad."

I kept driving. Another five minutes and I'd be home. But suddenly, I began remembering something. It was my senior year in college, a month before graduation.

I'd begun to send out job inquiries, typing them in my dorm. I'd learned you never make cover letters more than a page, so I didn't, but that presented a financial problem. I would buy 20-page boxes of the college's best stationery and only use the embossed page. The second, non-embossed pages were wasted. The job market was so tight that year I sent out scores of letters. At $10 a box, and at a time when I had no money, it pinched. And bothered me. Finally, I decided: Enough waste.

The next time I was in the college bookstore, I waited until the stationery aisle was empty. Then I picked up two boxes and switched half the paper so that one had all embossed pages and the other all second pages. I bought the one with the embossed pages, telling myself it wasn't really dishonest: the store was the one that had been unfair. It should have had that option to begin with. By now, I'd overpaid them four times for stationary boxes I only used half of; it was financial justice, not theft.

I got back to my dorm room feeling good about what I'd done and immediately sat down to type more cover letters. After only a few minutes, there was a knock on my door. As soon as I opened it, my legs went weak the way they do after a close call with a car accident.

It was Spence.

Spence was the nickname students used among ourselves for Chief Spencer, of college security. Next to him, looking stern, was the head of the bookstore.

"Excuse me," Spence said politely, "but can we see the box of stationery you just bought?"

Strange things go through your mind at such a moment. I considered saying, "What stationery?" I considered leaping through the window and running. Instead, I gave him the box, immediately admitting everything with a tortured explanation about needing a job and not having money for pages I didn't use.

But the store manager, who had the box by now, didn't seem to hear. He leafed through it, then shut it. "I thought so," he said.

Spence seemed sympathetic to me. He explained he would have to keep the box as evidence. And I would be hearing from the dean.

I did hear. As soon as I walked into the dean's office, I admitted everything, but he said this was a serious matter; stealing is stealing, whether $10 worth of stationery or a $1,000 television. What he said next almost made me cry. In most cases, he explained, students who steal are suspended for a semester. He would take it up with a judicial committee and let me know in a week.

Suspended? A month before graduation? My classmates would see me as a fool or a creep. My parents would kill me. I would have to return next year wearing a scarlet letter. I'd never get a job. It would ruin my life.

I prayed all week: "Please God, I'll do anything if you only don't let me get kicked out. Please, please, please."

The call came. I went to the dean's office. I could tell by his face that it was over for me.

"I'm sorry," he said, "but we've decided we have to level a serious punishment."

How could you do it to me, God?

"We'll be fining you $200."

I wanted to kiss him.

Now, 20 years later, here I was with my lollipop dilemma. And no, a 5 cent piece of candy taken innocently by a 2-year-old is not the same as a college student ripping off a store. But as I drove along, I began this weird fantasy: What if I get home, and find Spence waiting for me?

I stopped the car. I turned around. Then I drove back 15 long minutes, explained to the drug-store cashier what had happened and gave her a nickel. She thanked me, but looked at me like I was slightly mad. Still, in this life, you either learn a lesson or you don't.

Oh, there's a postscript to this story, and it's true. My senior year, I was back in the college bookstore a week after being fined, buying another box of stationery for more cover letters. I paid. I returned to my dorm room and opened it up.

It was all second pages. I'd bought the other box.

I never said a word.

As usual, the baggage pickup at Logan Airport in Boston was chaos. Finally, I spotted my luggage, loaded a cart and headed for the door. But I was soon blocked. An older woman, nicely dressed, was in front of me, speaking to a little boy. The child looked about 2.

"Excuse me," I said.

She didn't hear me. Her whole focus was on the boy. Struck me as rude. Awkwardly, I began steering around her, and then I heard her say it.

"You look very familiar to me," she said to the child. "I certainly hope I look familiar to you."

Now I paused, and observed, and it was clear the older woman did not look familiar to the boy. He shrank back. His expression said: "Who is this stranger?"

Then a thirtyish woman called the older woman "Mom." So she wasn't a stranger. She was the child's grandmother. And this brief scene said much about the way we now live.

In essence, she was saying: "I'm your grandmother, which you may not know because you live far away, and that means I miss many things, like your first steps and first words. But I'm your grandma. We are part of each other. And I hope, in time, while I am still here, and perhaps when I am no longer here, that I will mean something to you."

When I was a child, I don't think there were as many such scenes in airports. My surviving grandparents—two grandmothers—lived within miles. We saw them frequently. Sometimes it was fun and sometimes an obligation, but that's all right, that's normal. In time, I came to value having had two more people in my life who cared about what I did, and who I was.

But society is more mobile. Of the couples I know with children, only a few have all grandparents nearby. My own parents are two hours by airplane. That never used to bother me, but now leaves me feeling unconnected at times. We all want our children to be part of what we are, part of a greater family, and distance makes that difficult.

Of course, even if I lived closer, I'd hardly see them nightly, or weekly, perhaps not even monthly. But when six months pass and first steps and first words go by, I feel a hole. For my children. For myself.

There is a scene in a movie I first saw when I was childless, and didn't think twice about it, but saw it again not long ago on video, now having three children, and my reaction was very different.

It is a scene in a 19th-century Russian village. A father is embracing his grown daughter at a train stop. She is off to join her new husband far away and the father does not know when he will again see her, or his potential grandchildren.

He is strong for her as they embrace, but then, as the train pulls away, his chin quivers. And standing alone, he whispers out loud: "Goodbye, my life."

That is parenthood, and grandparenthood. If our role is to give children wings, we cannot resent it when they use them. If my own children find lives far away, I hope I will only encourage them.

And my grandchildren? A foreign thought right now. My kids are 8, 5 and 2. But if it happens someday, I know it's likely that their first steps and first words will happen far away.

Of course, this isn't 19th-century Russia. There are planes now. As long as I'm careful not to be a pain, I'm sure there will be visits. And I'm sure, no matter how much time goes by, that when I see them, they will look very familiar to me.

I hope I will look familiar to them.

WAX LIPS, VARSITY SWEATERS AND BURNING LEAVES

Things I Miss:
- The smell of burning leaves in Autumn.

- Wax lips, and wax bottles filled with that red, carcinogenic juice.

- Being an age when it was all right to openly eat Pez.

- I miss Sweet Tarts.

- And Fizzies, especially Rootin'-Tootin' Raspberry and Grumpy Grape.

- I miss Sean Connery as James Bond and Lucy having it out with Ricky.

- Hoss on Bonanza and Alfred Hitchcock looking at me with contempt and saying, ``Good evening."

- And Walter saying, "And that's the way it is."

- And Belushi shouting, "But noooo."

- I miss being so scared by The "Twilight Zone" and "Outer Limits" I couldn't sleep at night.

- I miss the Man From U.N.C.L.E.; America doesn't feel as safe without Napoleon Solo and Ilya Kuryakin.

- I miss girls wearing boys' varsity sweaters.

- Bob Dylan composing songs like "Blowin' in the Wind."

- I miss Laura Nyro.

- And go-karts and Kennedy half-dollars and bangs on girls.

- And hula hoops.

- I can't tell you how much I miss the smell of burning leaves in Autumn.

- I miss folk singing in coffee houses. And hootenannies.

- And Mad-Libs.

■ I miss Ouija boards—at a time when I still believed they were really driven by spirits.

■ I miss finding a surprise at the bottom of my cereal box. And my Cracker Jack box.

■ I miss vinyl record albums.

■ And Little Louie at short and Nellie Fox at second.

■ I miss hiding a transistor radio in my Fred Flinstone lunch bucket so could listen to the World Series in the school cafeteria.

■ I miss being able to buy a sneaker that was good for more than one sport.

■ I miss opening one of those plastic eggs to find a fresh wad of Silly Putty inside.

■ I miss the Golden Arches.

■ And Look magazine.

■ I miss the Twist and black high-top Keds.

■ And Jackie Gleason saying, "How sweet it is."

■ I miss paperboys on bicycles, enclosed phone booths and dime Hershey bars.

■ And I'm sorry, but I can't take it anymore. I don't care what the regulations say. Next Autumn, I'm going to go rake up a nice neat pile, and burn some leaves.

A CHRISTMAS STORY

I didn't know how I would be received; with resentment, I presumed. Here I was, a Westerner, wealthy by African standards, arriving at their sorry camp to write a story about a desert tribe brought down by famine.

They were Muslims, living in tents on the banks of the Niger River, in the north of Mali, not far from Timbuktu. They were part of the Turag tribe, once a people of means, prosperous nomads. But this year, 1984, the rains had stopped, and they'd been forced into a tent encampment, and their children were starving.

I was driven to their camp by a French doctor, grinding for hours in a Land Rover through the soft Sahara sand. The doctor dropped me off and made introductions, and that's when I thought I would be resented.

This journalist. This Westerner. Here for a story, and soon to be gone.

But rarely have I ever been so welcomed.

The group had a chief: Hamzata. He was well-educated, fluent in French. He had a mat laid out for me, and tea made, and he could not have been more embracing.

Still I could not have been lonelier. It was Christmas Eve, and I'd been traveling through Africa more than a month to write about famine. I'd begun in the heart of the misery, Ethiopia, moving on to a refugee camp in Sudan, then a swarming ghetto in Kenya where the drought-stricken had poured in from the countryside.

I remember being in a hotel room in Khartoum, watching a sappy movie, my eyes watering because being alone on the road can leave you emotionally fragile. Then I took a jetliner west across Africa, and Christmas music came on, and it made me long for home so badly it felt like a physical ache.

But I had this last stop to make.

Now I was here, Christmas Eve in the desert, and I was due to spend the whole night in this camp: The French doctor had said he couldn't pick me up until morning.

As I sat on the mat, I gripped the Swiss army knife in my pocket, adjusted my Ray Ban sunglasses and hunched into my L.L. Bean shirt, three of my most comfortable belongings, things I planned to save forever when I got home as simple treasures that helped me through my African trip.

I tried to picture home. In the States, people would be gathering for Christmas parties, then Christmas dinners. There would be fires and carols. And here I was.

In the center of the tents, a large blanket had been laid out. Dozens had gathered to receive me. The chief had me sit next to him. We began to talk, and as the hours went by, it taught me how well people who share little language can communicate if one of them has a story to tell. The chief told me his, how his tribe had once been wealthy, owning the desert, bringing teachers for their children as they wandered, journeying on camels and owning 1,000 cattle. He even showed me a photo album. But then the rains stopped, he said, and the cattle died and now they were kept alive, barely, by UNICEF. The people are hungry, he said. ``Les peuples est faim."

Then I managed to explain about the holiday. "Noel," I said. "Ce soir." Tonight. The chief's face brightened. He said he knew about Noel. That's when an extraordinary thing happened.

Although they were Muslims, to show honor for both myself and the holiday, the chief said they would celebrate this night. They had one goat left. I tried to protest but he told me the tribe would be insulted if I did not let them.

Soon the women began cooking, and I could smell a spicy stew. I took out my notebook to write thoughts, and right away, two men reached over with lanterns to help me. When the meal was ready, I tried to decline, but the chief motioned toward his people. Although they are hungry, he said, it would mean everything to them if I were to take part fully in this meal; sharing with strangers was their highest ethic.

Afterward the chief arranged a bed for me in his own room-sized tent. Lying there in the darkness, across our cultures, we talked into the night until I faded into a deep, restful sleep.

At midmorning I was with the chief when we heard the sound of an approaching Land Rover; my ride. That's when it happened.

He told me to wait, then emerged from his tent with a silk turban and placed it in my hands. For you, he said. ``Noel joyeux."

At that, I gave him my sunglasses, my Swiss Army knife and my shirt, leaving myself in a turtleneck after the cold night. "For you," I said.

Still wearing the turban, I climbed into the Jeep. A dozen years later, I can still picture the whole tribe waving goodbye.

I have never had a better Christmas.

OH SHAME, OH MISPRONUNCIATION

I was sharing the newspaper with my wife the other morning when she came across a story she felt needed more attention. She told me it should have been displayed more prominently.

"Right," I answered. Then I tried to impress her by adding a fancy phrase. "Kind of bring it out in bass relief."

That's how I pronounced it: "bass" relief. Like the fish.

My wife stared at me.

"You mean bas relief," she said, pronouncing it "bah." As in Scrooge's favorite phrase. That happens to be the correct way. Only I never knew that.

It reminded me of an affliction I've had for years: I suffer from mispronunciation.

Until I was about 25, I thought that trash along the side of the road was referred to as "debriss." It was my misfortune to be set straight by my older brother, Hugh. His whole life, he's taken great joy in reminding me of my shortcomings.

"Debriss?" he repeated. "That's de-bree, simpleton." Which is another problem faced by those of us who suffer from mispronunciation. People who hear us do it love to turn the knife.

Until I was 30, I thought there was such a word as MY-zuld. As in, "He was MY-zuld by a con artist."

"God, you're hopeless," my older brother finally corrected. "The word is misled." Pronounced miss-led.

Then there was the word "berserk." For most of my life, I pronounced it "burr-sick," somehow having interpreted in my younger mind that berserk derived from the idea of a mule, or some other animal, going wild because it had too many burrs.

Similarly, I always thought the term was laxadaisical, based on someone who was lax. I once thought you pronounced colonel as if referring to a specialist of a certain body part. After graduating college, I couldn't wait to make my debutt as a full-time journalist. I only recently learned it's the cavalry that rides to the rescue, not the calvary. Same with that word for being delighted with something—most of my life, I thought it was r'VELL, not REH'vul. And if melee is pronounced may-lay, they should spell it that way; I would have avoided a lifetime of making it sound like the worms I once fed my lizards.

It's a comfort to find there are other people who suffer from mispronunciation. A few years ago, I was with a college friend who worked as a nuclear engineer. We were talking about someone we knew whose personality changed depending on whom he was with.

"The guy's a real shamalon," said my friend.

I paused. "What's a shamalon?"

"You know, those lizards that change colors."

I took a brief poll to see what other words trip up adults. One guy remembered having visited YO-s'might Park on a trip out west. A woman had a friend who liked the warmth from a fireplace hurth. Another referred to a chemise as a camiss, while several thought a chamois shirt is pronounced sha-moy. And almost everyone thinks the person hired to watch a bank's books is pronounced COMP-troller, not controller.

Many people seem to have trouble with the word "draught;" the suspicion persists that it's pronounced drowt. "I just freeze up," one man told me. "I go around it: 'May I have a beer from that barrel thing.' Anyway I can avoid it."

Another has the same trouble with trough. He suspects it may be pronounced trow, but he's not sure, so he avoids it. "If I ever saw a thirsty horse," he said, "I'd just say, 'There; that thing full of water over there—go drink it.' "

Menus may be the most intimidating of all. It's a world filled with crudities, foy grass, and that difficult trilogy: beef borganon, tornadoes of beef, and beef au juice.

Finally, there's my most embarrassing mispronunciation. I remember being in a childbirth class when the teacher told us to all lie on the floor.

"In a prostate position?" I asked. Frankly, I still can't keep prostate and prostrate clear.

But I'd like to close with an observation:

The burr-sick colon-ul r'velled in bass relief after he my-zuld the laxadaisical calvary into lying prostate next to the debriss.

You could probably pronounce that better. And I've learned to. But the way I just wrote it will always sound truest to my ear.

🕐

YOU HAVE ENDED MY SEARCH

I was trying to ignore that this was Paris. I'd come here for business, to do interviews for a book, and wanted to focus on that alone. The plane and hotel would be costing $3,000 from the advance, so it was important to squeeze all I could out of this week.

By phone, you urged me not to be so obsessive, to take at least one evening, walk the Left Bank, revisit the places we'd discovered together. I told you I couldn't. I would need my nights to go over interview notes, looking for holes to plug before my plane home. My time this week would be too short for leisure. The only way to get $3,000 of work done would be to ignore that this was Paris.

But then came tonight.

I'd just finished my last interview and decided to walk to the Metro. I did not realize how close I was to the Seine. One block, and I was there, right at the Ile de Cite, where the book stalls line the banks. I stopped to browse, telling myself it would be for just a moment.

But I lingered for more than a moment. Then it began to rain, a cold, fall, Paris rain. It was an excuse to find a cab, so I crossed the Quai Montebello, trying to wave one down, though not successfully. After 10 minutes, chilled and wet, I decided to find an awning. As I headed for a row of storefronts, I realized where I was.

Remember how we found Shakespeare & Company together? Remember it—Hemingway's old bookstore, still venerably preserved in a disarray of shelves that allows you to find things you aren't looking for, as we did that one night.

I decided to pause, spending a good a hour there, and wanted to make it longer, but I couldn't shake the chill. All right; finally, to the hotel.

Then I realized what was next door. I think, if we had a favorite restaurant from that week in Paris, it was La Bucherie. And here it was. And a fire was going in a big central hearth, with the same black Lab lying next to it. The tables were set in white linen, each with a vase of flowers.

That's when I knew the book project would have to wait. This night, I would give to myself.

I ordered dinner, not quite sure what I was ordering, just as I did when we were here. I pointed at the menu, saying, "Qu'est que c'est," and then, after the waiter trilled a fast burst of French I didn't understand, I nodded anyway to show him I was a sophisticate, saying "Ah, je comprends, c'est bon." Even though I didn't comprends.

But that was all right. Anything he brought would be fine—just as it was fine that I was avoiding work. All that mattered was that every now and then in life, you get a perfect moment.

You know about that, don't you? Like that moment you told me about on the island, when you got snowed in, and your only way to get around was cross- country skis. You told me how you would hold onto the memory of those few days forever. We agreed that such times are what it's about, finding moments in life when everything is perfect.

There in La Bucherie, I took out a pad and pen to write you of how I'd found such a moment in Paris; how I had the whole restaurant to myself, with a fire going, and a bowl of French bread, and Notre Dame looming beyond the window, washed by the rain. A perfect moment.

But it wasn't perfect.

After dinner, I went back into Shakespeare's, and found another book I wasn't looking for, but that wasn't perfect either. By then, the rain had stopped, so I walked to the center of the Petit Pont, with the Seine below, and Notre Dame above it. But still, I couldn't make the moment happen for me. I could not make Paris happen.

And I know why I couldn't.

There is a scene at the end of the movie, "Out of Africa." The woman who would later write under the name of Isak Dinesen was preparing to leave her coffee farm in the Ngong Hills, possibly forever. In doing so, she would also be leaving her soulmate, Denys Finch-Hatton. Up until then, he had always been a man who treasured solitude above all things. But now, as they said goodbye, he told her something.

"You've ruined it for me," I remember him saying.

She asked what he meant.

"Being alone," he said. "You've ruined it."

As you have for me.

It is something we all search for—even those of us who think we are strong. We search for someone who will make it hard for us to be alone.

ALSO BY MARK PATINKIN

An African Journey, 1985.
The Silent War (with Ira Magaziner), 1989.
The Rhode Island Dictionary, 1993.
The Rhode Island Handbook, 1994.